ACHIEVEMENT IN SOCIAL STUDIES

ACHIEVEMENT IN SOCIAL STUDIES

Dr. Digumarti Bhaskara Rao
Ms. Kandru Vijaya
Ms. Chennupati Sridevi
R.V.R. College of Education
Guntur—522 006
Andhra Pradesh
(India)

DISCOVERY PUBLISHING HOUSE
New Delhi—110 002 (INDIA)

Reprinted - 2019

First Published - 1995

ISBN: 978-81-7141-281-5

Achievement in Social Studies

Published by:

DISCOVERY PUBLISHING HOUSE PVT. LTD.
4383/4B, Ansari Road, Darya Ganj
New Delhi-110 002 (India)
Phone: +91-11-23279245, 23253475; 43596065
E-mail: discoverybooksindia@gmail.com
discoverypublishinghouse@gmail.com
web: www.discoverypublishinggroup.com

Printed at:
Infinity Imaging Systems
Delhi

FOREWORD

Social Studies has been introduced into the school curriculum to help children develop an insight into human relationships, social values and attitudes, and to enable them to appreciate the rich and varied cultural heritage. It deals with the web of relationships that develop among people and between people and environment. It also provides explanatory experiences in and out of the classroom to prepare the pupils for effective citizenship.

Social Studies is made one of the core subjects in India after the recommendations of educational commissions and policies. The subject Social Studies is studied from the very beginning of schooling and because of this the children must acquire a sound knowledge of it to apply in various situations at need.

Examination is one such need which measures and evaluates the understanding of Social Studies by the students. The students have to face it confidently and reach upto the expected level of performance. The researchers have taken this aspect, measured the achievement of secondary school students, and evaluated the associated factors of Social Studies achievement. As the research findings are not so encouraging, the entire educational machinery must put in all their efforts to enhance the academic achievement.

I congratulate the researchers for their efforts and request the readers to look carefully into the problems associated with Social Studies achievement in order to promote academic achievement.

Dr. K.R.S. Sambasiva Rao
Nagarjuna University
Nagarjuna Nagar
Andhra Pradesh (India)

PREFACE

As the children grow toward maturity, they learn two great lessons—firstly, they learn that their unique and individual qualities are cherished, and secondly, they learn that they live in a social world that imposes limits on what they can do. The Social Studies seeks to help them strike a reasoned balance between self-centered personal development and unthinking acquiescence to the whims of others.

As pursuers of Social Studies are encouraged to work out a reasonable compromise between personal desires and social responsibilities, teachers of Social Studies attempt to broaden the range of their interests. By exposing children to people, places and issues beyond the parochial limits of the school and the community, the Social Studies education empasizes the interdependence nature of the human community.

As an entree to stimulate student interest in Social Studies, it is desirable to connect instruction to personal experiences and interests of children. This implies a need for the teachers to diagnose child characteristics in order to identify interests and possible basic misconceptions. Given this information, lessons can be constructed that take advantage of identified student characteristics.

As realised by many Social Studies educationists, the programmes of Social Studies, should enhance the students' abilities to understand, analyze, bring information to bear, to choose, to resolve, and to act wisely. Competence in the individual, not dogma, is the supreme objective.

As our students are lagging behind the expected level of performance, we suggest to follow and implement the methods that come in our way to help achieve well.

Dr. D. Bhaskara Rao
Ms. K. Vijaya
Ms. C. Sridevi

ACKNOWLEDGEMENTS

We are thankful to Dr. K.R.S. Sambasiva Rao, Nagarjuna University, for expressing his views in the foreword.

We are thankful to Dr. L. Rathaiah, Chairman, Vignan Vidyalayas Ltd., Hyderabad; Mr. C.V.L Narasimha Rao, Secretary and Correspondent, Sri Prakash Group of Educational Institutions, Tuni; Mr. P. Koteswara Rao, J.K.C. College, Guntur, Mr. P. Narasimha Rao, Nagarjuna University; Mr. M. Nageswara Rao, J.K.C. College; and Dr. B.K. Manmohan Singh, Osmania University, Hyderabad for their moral support in every academic effort.

We are also thankful to Mr. C. Venkateswarlu, Mr. M.V.S. Koteswara Rao, Mr. G. Nageswara Rao, Mr. G.P. Ranga Rao, Mr. N. Murali, Mr. N. Satya Narayana, Mr. J. Ravindra Babu, Mr. V. Venkateswara Rao, Mr. A. Sudhakara Rao, Mr. J. Venkata Rao, Mr. M. Janardhana Rao, Mr. U. Venkata Subbaiah, Mr. N.S.R. Prasad, Mr. Y. Jaya Sankara Prasad, Mrs. G. Usha Rani, Mrs. M. Krishna Sri, Mrs. V. Vijaya Lakshmi and Ms. B. Veena Kumari for their united cooperation.

Bhaskara Rao
Vijaya
Sridevi

CONTENTS

CONTENTS

1

INTRODUCTION

The school is an important social institution which has to discharge its responsibility in the content of the purposes that a society desires to fulfil through it. One of our national goals is the establishment of a vital democracy through the development of an enlightened and responsible citizenry imbibed with an abiding faith in democratic principles and processes. The school, undoubtedly, has to play an important role in the achievement of this aim, and a large share of that responsibility is to be shouldered by the subject which goes by the name of Social Studies.

Current educational theory holds that the school is responsible for the education of the child. Nevertheless, it is also true that particular subjects must assume primary responsibility for the realization of one or more of ten general aims of education. Social Studies is then a specific subject which has a primary responsibility in helping to develop a body of devoted, active, well-informed and discriminating citizens, who participate effectively in the affairs of the locality, the state, and the nation.

Social Studies is the field of study which deals with man, his relations with other men and his environment. Its content is drawn from several Social Sciences and bears a direct relationship with the purposes for which it is taught. Broadly speaking, these purposes include an understanding of human relations, knowledge of the environment, dedication to the basic principles and values of the society in which it is taught, and a commitment to participation in the processes through which that society is maintained and improved.

In other words, Social Studies seeks to develop in our future citizens an understanding of and an allegiance to cherished values of Indian society and also a fervent desire to strive for the betterment of present ways of life and social institutions. To do all this, it aims at imparting relevant knowledge and its utilization.

One of the primary concerns of Social Studies, therefore, is to promote an understanding of man's way of living, his basic needs,. the activities in which he engages to meet his needs—social, economic, culture and political—and the institutions he has developed.

Another dominant purpose behind the teaching of Social Studies, as has been said above, is to commit the learner to the basic principles and purposes for the society, in which he lives. When that society is governed by democratic principles, as ours is, the commitment means no more than the inculcation in the mind of the learner of an abiding faith in the democratic ideal. This must not be taken to mean indoctrination, in the sense of teaching specific and definite answers to the day-to-day problems of the society or of the world. But it does not mean the promotion of fundamental values and processes of a democratic society such as open-mindedness exercising of independent judgement, and participation in activities designed to influence public policy.

Over and above this, Social Studies keeps before itself the all pervading educational purpose of developing a rational and scientific approach to social problems and issues. This can be fulfilled only by fostering in the learners the ability to discern the point at an issue to shift from the relevant to irrelevant, to marshal ideas in a logical sequence and to express themselves with lucidity and effectiveness.

To repeat, the term Social Studies is used to designate that school subject or that area of school curriculum which deals with human relationships. Therefore, the content of Social Studies deals with the physical and social environment. The over all, objective of social studies, therefore, would be the development of a well-informed, intelligent person, who is alive to current problems and is keen to accept responsibilities as a citizen. For the welfare of all, he understands the concepts that describe and explain the human society, that are developing insights, skills, and moral qualities, which are so desirable in a democratic society.

ORIGIN OF SOCIAL STUDIES

A comfortable life in any society needs some restrictions - Do's and Don'ts. Every one has to respect the movements of neighbours and mould his movements in such a fashion that they shall not bother others. These are called limitations—an essential part of any civilized life.

In earlier times these limitations were taught by "Conventional Wisdom," *i.e.*, elders taught the youngers these limitations. This knowledge of limitation was passed from one generation to the succeeding generation. Oral transmissions, ceremonial occasions were used for this purpose. Since the skills that were required for survival were the same, this scheme worked very well.

World is changing at a faster rate. New generations started facing new challenges. The accelerating change in the social, technical spheres demanded new social rules that were not known to preceding generations. New ideas often challenging old ones, demand for new social and political structures, etc., necessitate a different treatment to "social life". The result is a separate branch of human knowledge called "Social Studies", also called "Social Sciences", when studied at a higher level.

In the beginning—in colonial era—the study of Social Studies was mostly confined to moral concern with some reference to social issues. Subject matter draw heavily upon insights from religious books. The acceptability of behaviour was moulded and the basis of religious morality.

The American Revolution put a break on this, though the influence of biblical spirit pervaded the authors of the Social Studies text books who devoted considerable attention to topics like "Good breeding" and "Proper manners". Instruction of civic manners made its entry into Social Studies.

Important changes in the study of Social Studies were being taken place since nineteenth century. During the first half of 19th century, 'History' became important as separate subject in secondary schools and 'Geography' followed it. These changes were significant, because they brought a new orientation to Social Studies. The perspective morality served up to students within the frameworks of these disciplines began to give way to more emphasis on contents that were more purely historical or geographic in nature.

In the second half of 19th century 'Political Science' was introduced. 1920s saw the introduction of two more important subjects, i.e., Economics and Sociology. During this period instructors, became increasingly interested in issues relating to the personal development of students. For the first time in the history of school education Social Studies programmes attempted to promote the personal development of students rather than in terms of the subject or topics to which students would be exposed. This was well defined by Beared, when he said that the programmes of the Social Studies should enhance the abilities of the students to understand, analyze, bring information to bear, to choose, to resolve, and to act wisely. According to him development of competence in the individual but not dogmer shall be the supreme objective of instructors and authors.

Another development in the history of Social Studies that deserves a special mention is the introduction of new course in America in 1920s. The title of the new course is "Problems of Democracy". This was a hybrid course and drew contents from various subjects, like Economics, Civics, Geography, etc.

Now, the study of Social Studies occupies very important place at school level. Each and every student was taught the essential nature of various social problems ranging from environment to social behaviour, thus helping the students to acquire knowledge on them and their environment.

SOCIAL STUDIES IN INDIA

Though Social Studies found its place in the school curriculum in 1937, its content was a part of education in India since the vedic period. A good part of the curriculum since vedic period was devoted to the regulation of social behaviour, ethics, need for morals in social life, etc. The history of Social Studies could be divided into 5 periods in India, *viz.*,

1. Vedic Period
2. Post-Vedic period
3. Muslim period
4. The British period.
5. Post-independence period.

The Vedic Period

The period covers the period of Vedas, Upanishads and other great Indian epics. Philosophical orientation was the purpose of education during this time. The emancipation of the soul was looked as the ultimate aim of education. Students were taught the necessity of keeping the mundane pleasures away from life. Religion was considered as the only way to achieve this. Thus, the education was religious. As Mukerjee rightly commented, "learning in India through the ages had been prized and pursued not for its own sake..... but for the sake and as a part of religion". Mukti or Emancipation was the Goal. According to Rawat, "Chitta-Vrtitti-Mirodha" or "the control of mental activities connected with the so-called concrete world"

Besides Mukti, Emancipation and Religious Philosophy some other important aspects were also found their place in the curriculum of Vedic period. They are :

1) Development of the personality of the student.
2) Training in the skills of citizenship and social life.
3) Imparting technical and craft education.
4) Inculcating the ideal of simple living and high thinking.
5) Development of qualities in intellectual capabilities and free expression.
6) Education on nature and environment.

Sarat Chandran who worked on education in Valmiki Ramayana identified the following major aspects of education :

1) To develop an all-round personality of the child—mental, Physical, moral aesthetic, spiritual, etc.
2) To make students fit for the discharge of their varnasrama dharmas.

3) To inculcate a sense of truthfulness, honesty and integrity.

The Post-Vedic Period

This period starts from the Buddhism and ends with the invasion and settlement of Muslim rulers in India. Buddhism and Jainism, two contemporary and most important religions of India, and their education systems aimed at Nirvana (salvation). Religious discourse was the central to the curriculum though other subjects like logic, accountancy, philosophy, etc., were also taught.

Like Buddhist education the ultimate aim of Jainist education was also salvation. Besides salvation its purposes included importing right knowledge, right philosophy and right character, necessary for the all-round development of the student.

The Muslim Period

Muslims conquered India and established their empire in eighteenth century. They introduced a new system of education. The aims of their education were : **1**. Propagation of Islam, **2**. Islamic social morals, **3**. Material progress, and **4**. Political support.

There was no Government structure to overlook the education. Throughout the Muslim period educational institutions were maintained with the help of philanthropist donations. Teachers enjoyed complete freedom and prepared syllabus, educational schemes, etc., of their own. According to Ahmad, the Islamic education was divided into three stages—primary, Secondary and Higher. However, Khashavis maintains that there were only two stages-Primary and Higher education.

The aim of primary education was to teach the pupil the knowledge of the alphabet and religious prayers. The aim of the secondary stage was to teach the Persian grammar and literature. Higher education consisted of logic, philosophy, law, astrology arithmetic, history, geography, medicine, agriculture, etc., besides grammar and literature.

The British Period

The roots of the modern Indian education were sown by the Britishers. Though the purpose of the education was entirely different, the structrue, the stages, structural arrangements, etc., were the contribution of the British in modern India.

Unlike the Muslims who conquered and made India as their home, the British conquered India only to exploit its natural resources. So, naturally their interest was not in development of India. They used every institution to exploit India, and education has no exemption. More over, the manpower available in Great Britain was not sufficient to control a vast country like India. So, they wanted to use the services in military, and in administration of the Indians to control India. The ultimate result was introducing such type of educational system which will ensure a committed pro-British elite educated group of Indians. This was made crystal-clear in the following communique by lord Macaulay, the chief architect of Indian education system.

"We must at present do our best to form a class who may be interpreters between us and the millions we govern, a class of persons, Indian in blood and colour, but English in taste, in opinion, in morals, and in intellect. And that the great object of the British Government ought to be the promotion of European literature and Science among the natives of India, and that all the funds appropriated for the purpose of education would be employed on English education alone".

Initially, the British did not show much interest in education of India. Much of their time was preoccupied with wars and business. As Deva Raj Dutt rightly observed, "the British were neither involved in Indian education nor did they have any clear-cut policy. They were busy in consolidating their political power in the interest of their mother country".

This non-involvement by the British government was compensated by the Christian missionaries. who started schools in various parts of the British India. Their purpose was also mainly to propagate the message of the Christ.

Later, the British government also started involving itself in education and its organization, but it was a policy of downward filtration (education of few or only elite) instead of man education. The reason was obvious - It did not want to educate all Indians and it wanted to educate any few, who will act as buffer

At the levels of Primary, Secondary and Higher education, the British wanted to copy the system of education that was prevailing in Britain. The syllabus, examination, evaluation, etc., were the simple replicas of the British system of education.

The Post-Independent Period

India became independent on August 15, 1947. Thus it got an opportunity to use the system of education for its own development. It set the goal of universal, free and compulsory education. It realized that universalization of education is the only alternative to raise its potential in industry and agriculture.

But, unfortunately, there was not much change in the system of education, except that Whites were replaced by the Browns in the office. The academicians working in this area are of the opinion that a complete and thorough re-orientation of the entire attitude towards education is necessary to achieve the goals that are set by the fathers of the Constitution.

By and large, Social Studies seeks to faster the objectives, that a general education programme attempts to attain and, therefore, it is to be regarded as an indispensable part of general education.

MEANING OF SOCIAL STUDIES

Social Studies is the offspring of Social Sciences, that is primarily concerned with the social aspects of human behaviour. The very name itself describes the meaning of the field- 'social' means concerning society, and 'studies' implies areas to be learned. Hence, Social Studies is an area that is to be learned about Society and its problems. There is no agreement on the definition of Social Studies. Various committees, commissions and scholars defined it differently.

The national Council of Educational Research and Training, gave the meaning of Social Studies as "A field of study which deals with man, his relations with other men and his environment....... an understanding of human relationships, knowledge of the environment, dedication to the basic principles and values of the society in which it is taught, and a commitment to participate in the processes through which that society is maintained and improved".

In the words of Wesley and Wronski the term "Social studies indicates materials whose content and term are predominantly social. The Social Studies utilized substantive and procedural aspects of the Social Sciences for pedagogical purpose."

The definition given by James High is as follows, "Most simply stated, the Social Studies are the school mirrors of the scholarly findings of the Social Sciences. Such data as social scientists may gather is integrated and simplified to appropriate levels of expression for children in all the grades."

The above definitions reveal that the contents, methods and organization of Social Studies are derived directly from purposes for which they are taught which include an understanding of human relationship, knowledge of the environment, dedication to the basic principles and values of the society in which Social Studies is taught, and a commitment to the processes through which that society is maintained and improved. The above constitute what may be called Social Studies.

Thus, Social Studies is an embracing subject in the sense that it touches all aspects of human life. It derives from the social science—a body of content focussed upon the activities man undertakes as he meets his fundamental needs. One of the primary concerns of social Studies is to promote an understanding of man's ways of living, his basic needs and the activities in which he engages to meet his needs- social, economic, cultural, and political- and the institutions he has developed. Therefore, Social Studies is a study of the society in general and the community in particular.

NATURE OF SOCIAL STUDIES

There is a question on the nature of Social Studies. Whether it is a Science or an Art? Many scholars were hesitant to place that in any one of these two compartments, and consider Social Studies as both a Science and an Art.

Some thinkers viewed Civics as a Science. If the broader meaning of the word 'science' is considered, social studies can be called a Science. All the human knowledge can be broadly called Science, when Science is defined as a body of systematized knowledge, and its function is to establish a relationship between cause and effect and deduce generalizations. In the words of Garner, "Science is a knowledge relating to a particular subject acquired by a systematic observation, experience or study which have been co-ordinated, systematized and classified. "Science is, thus, a collection of facts of a particular type. The facts are classified and systematized on the basis of their degree of accuracy. Conveniently, Science can be classified into three groups, *viz.*, abstract, natural and social sciences. Abstract Sciences are concerned with mental concepts and ideas but not with things so much, for *e.g.*., Logic and Philosophy. Natural Sciences include both Physical Sciences which deal with physical phenomena such as Physics, Chemistry, Geology and Astronomy, and the Biological Sciences, which relate to life in its various forms and manifestations, such as Botany, Zoology, etc. And Social Sciences include all those Sciences which study social life in its various forms. As it is done in the case of a Science, Social Studies also deduces its laws on the basis of observation, experiment, analysis, etc., although its laws are not exact and definite. We, therefore, hold that Social Studies is a Science. But, Classification of facts and the formulation of laws that are mutually consistent and universally valid upon the basis of rational judgements-constitute the essential aim of modern Science. But social phenomena are perpetually undergoing change and are difficult to control. Social Studies, it must be admitted, can not be an exact Science.

Social Studies is considered as an Art because Art is defined as "human skill as opposed to nature". However, Art in its broader sense, also implies the practical application of Science to real life. Social Studies is not merely a theoretical enquiry to get knowledge about social life and institutions simply for the sake of knowledge, it's purpose is to create an active and intelligent interest among the citizens to secure a better life. Hence, Social Studies can be considered as an art of living as a good citizen.

We can say that Social Studies is both a Science and an Art in the sense that it investigates conditions and seeks to apply the results of its investigations to the furtherance of human welfare.

SOCIAL STUDIES AND SOCIAL SCIENCES

Social Studies is a field that studies human relationships. But, often the term Social Studies has been treated as a synonym to Social Sciences. Yet, there is a considerable difference between these two. Despite the fact that both Social Studies and Social Sciences deal with human relationships, they differ in their scope. Narration and probe are the scope of Social Studies and Social Sciences respectively. Moreover, they differ in their standards and purposes.

Generally speaking, Social Sciences concentrate on investigation, research and solution to Social problems, where as Social Studies is more or less of a descriptive type when the information is truly presented.

The Social Sciences are concerned with the areas of knowledge dealing with the relationships of human beings with each other and with their natural environment, i.e. with the society. They include such areas as history, economics, political science, anthropology, sociology, geography, etc. The Social Sciences present the story of human affairs from the past to our contemporary life. And the Social Studies may be considered in terms of knowledge drawn from the Social Sciences and contemporary life for instructional purposes in aiding the youth in becoming a good citizens.

Thus, the Social Studies as a field of enquiry aids students through sound knowledge, information and the functional experiences which are essential to the building of basic values, desirable habits and accepted attitudes and worthwhile skills basic to effective citizenship; where as the subject matter of Social Sciences can be used in understanding trends, solving problems and revealing the past as a means toward better understanding of the present. Understanding of the Social Sciences gives a broader knowledge and a complete picture of the growth of modern civilization. In fact, today's civilization with all its complexities needs the fruits of the Social Sciences for better understanding. And the fundamental test of the Social Sciences is accuracy, reliability and eventual social utility, where as the fundamental test of the Social Studies is instructional utility. Though, the Social Studies are also under obligations to be accurate and reliable they automatically meet this requirement by including faithful portions or versions of Social Sciences.

Generally, the term Social Sciences is applied to the research materials about human beings and their interrelationships. A report on the political parties, a monograph on business cycles, and an analysis of the budget and its affect on the State economy, etc., are the examples of materials, which belong to the Social Sciences are concerned with the detailed, systematic, and logical study of human relationships.

The materials of Social Sciences neither necessarily technical, difficult, remote nor they necessarily popular and easy. Their obligation is to the standards of research rather than to the psychological aptitudes of prospective readers and to society as a whole rather than to a set of students.

The materials of Social Sciences may or may not be suitable for instructional purposes at the college level and are less likely to be useful at high or elementary school levels. The Social Sciences are the storehouses of knowledge, particularly scientific social knowledge.

In contrast, the Social Studies are designed primarily for instructional purposes. They are those portions or aspects of Social Sciences that have been selected and adopted for use in the school or in other instructional situations. The term Social Studies indicates materials whose content as well as aim is predominantly social. The Social Studies are the Social Sciences, but simplified for pedagogical purposes and consist of materials of instruction. Hence, we can say that Social Sciences represent an adult approach, while the Social Studies represent a child-centered approach.

From the above description, it can be said that the Social Studies summarizes what has already been ascertained. Hence, the primary purpose of this field is to disseminate information. So, it has no contemporary reference. On the other hand, Social Sciences have social applications and are contemporary. They mean the present conditions and problems, and recognize the ultimate social purposes of the people. Hence Social Sciences are useful not only to present generations, but also to the future generations.

The focus and emphasis of both are different. For example, when a student studies geography as a Social Science, he has to focus his attention on the methods of Geography, the tools and concepts of the subject and knowledge which will provide a basis for further specialization at a later stage. The student studying Geography as part of the Social Studies programme should focus attention on using ideas and concepts from Geography to understand man and various parts of the world and how geographical factors influence relationships between groups of men and nations today.

Moreover, Social Studies and Social Science differ in their scope. The Social Sciences are far larger than Social Studies. Social Sciences observe a phenomenon, verify, measure and quantify the same phenomenon. The basic purpose of any Social Science is to discover universal and everlasting truths. Social Studies do not indulge in any exercise that involves observation and verification. They do not probe into any social event. Social Studies simply present a phenomenon as it was accepted by the majority. Questions like 'why', 'how' and 'when' are kept beyond the scope of Social Studies. Where as, Social Sciences start with 'why'.

Further more, both differ in their aim also. The primary aim of Social Studies is instructional utility where as Studies primarily meant to the formal groups, but Social Sciences were interested in the society at large.

To conclude, we can say that there is no hard and past line separating Social Sciences and Social Studies. At the primary classes, where gradual unfoldment of the total environment-physical, social and cultural-is needed, Social Studies is to be taught. As the student becomes a competent investigator and interpreter of raw data in the Middle and Secondary stages and later, he emerges from the Social Studies into the Social Science.

BRANCHES OF SOCIAL STUDIES

Social Studies represents a broad and composite institutional area, which deals with a variety of man's needs and problems so as to make the child acquaint with his past and present geographical and social environment. It draws the information from different Social Science such as History, Geography, Civics,

Economics, etc., in order to unfold gradually the total environment of the child with reference to the physical, social and cultural elements. Different facets of man's experiences are included in the content of Social Studies, to give a comprehensive idea of human society to the child.

History, Geography, Civics and Economics are to be taught in Social Studies so that the vital elements are fused in a way which are relevant for entertaining and amplifying children's day-to-day economic, social and civic experiences, and to develop an insight into human relationships, social values and attitudes.

Each branch has its own contribution to the aim of Social Studies teaching. History makes an attempt to answer the questions how our present life has come into being and what was the quality of inheritance of which we are heirs. It gives the youth an insight, appreciation and understanding of historical and cultural problems. Geography trains the future citizens to imagine accurately the conditions of the great world stage so that they may think sensibly about political and social and practical problems in the world. Civics provides realistic and first hand knowledge and experience, leading to improvement of daily living in home, school and community and the eventual participation by pupils in the life of the country in a democratic manner. Economics makes the child familiar with the multifarious economic activities and the economic structure of the society which would help him to meet his basic needs and offer him various channels at the close of his school career. It is to help the child know the natural resources of his country and how he can make maximum use of them to improve conditions of living: the necessary complementarity between production and consumption; and how human goals can be achieved through planning. Let us see the continuation of each branch.

History

History is the oldest of Social Sciences. It is that branch of knowledge which has for its object the ascertaining recording and explaining of facts and events of the past. Literally, the word 'History' is derived from the Greek word 'Historia', which means inquiry or, more specifically, knowledge through inquiry. N C E R T opined history as the scientific study of past happenings in all their aspects, in the life of a social group, in the light of present happenings.

The origin of History can be found in the myths and traditions of early primitive peoples, handed down from the generation to generation. From the days when Greece flourished and made her contributions to civilization the term "History" has been used. Although historical tradition goes back into antiquity, the Greeks were the first writers of history in the accepted sense of the term. Herodotus was regarded as the "Father of History".

The mass of facts consisting of past events and including the activities of nations, societies, and civilizations, written from varying points of view and differing motives makes up the body of knowledge called History. The economic, social and cultural life of mankind won the core of the History in the later years. So the subject matter was rigid and lifeless. Changes that have occurred since the beginning of the present century have enlarged the boundaries of History, as taught in the secondary school, to include social, economic, industrial, scientific and cultural aspects in addition to the political phases. School history is to some degree also becoming interpretative rather than merely descriptive.

History occupies a central place in the Social Studies programme of the secondary school of today, because many educators behind that it was an excellent subject for training the memory and for the formal discipline. History was also believed to be in inculcating morals, in developing religious life, in inspiring patriotism, in training for citizenship, and in providing for the profitable use of leisure time. Its introduction into the school was evidence of the beginning of a broadening view of the purpose of education and the extention of its functions.

Geography

Geography is the science that studies the elements of the physical environment in which a community lives and the effect such environment has on the individual and social life of the community. It studies, for example, the climate, the mineral and agricultural resources of a country.

The word Geography originated from the Greek roots 'Gee' and 'graphein', which mean 'Earth' and 'to write' respectively. Hence, Geography is the science that describes the

Earth's surface. Geography is concerned with the arrangements of things and with the association of things that distinguish one area from another.

Geography is one of the oldest studies of mankind, which was in existence from the times of Ptolemy and Stralo, who were considered as early geographers. However, the credit of giving a systematic treatment of the subject matter of Geography goes to Immanuel Kant. In the modern period, Geography laid emphasis on the relationships and cultures of peoples of different areas and country, and the subject became increasingly an explanation of the reactions between man and his environment instead of an array of facts and definitions. Thus, modern Geography became an explanatory study showing how the environment has conditioned and influenced.

Geography is an important subject to train future citizens to imagine accurately the conditions of the great world stage, and to help the student to think about the would around. The aims for the subject should lead to an understanding and appreciation of how people live and work; how the environment affects their lives, ideas, and customs; and how those in one region affect those of another. The study of Geography promotes a better understanding among individuals, groups and the nations of the world.

Systematic Geography may be conveniently subdivided into Physical Geography—it includes climatology, hydrography, and the study of land forms; Biogeography - the geography of soils and of plant, animal, and human population; Human Geography - the Geography of the economic, political, and social activities; Historical Geography - concerned primarily with the human geography of the past and is of importance because so many of the present spatial patterns owe much to earlier ones.

Civics

Civics is the science of citizenship. It studies man as a citizen. The activities, qualities, rights, and duties of a citizen and the position he occupies in the society and state are discussed in Civics, Broadly spreading, the study of Civics should be considered as the study of the citizen as a member of the city, of the country and of humanity at large.

The term 'Civics' is derived from two Latin words 'civitas' which means 'city' or 'city-state' and 'civis' which means 'citizen'. Thus it is to be understood that Civics is originally a study of man as a member of the city. It is believed that cities were the places of civilization, which is an advanced stage in the social life of man. According to the Oxford Dictionary, Civics is that part of political science which is concerned with the rights and duties of citizenship. The Encyclopedia of Britannica defines Civics as the name given to the study of citizenship and government. In the words Civics is the science and philosophy of citizenship.

The place that Civics holds in the curriculum of the secondary school today is an important one. From 1930s slow progress was made in introducing the subject into the schools as a compulsory one. Though, civics was considered as a subject by 1890, it was taught only in a few schools. In those times, the subject of Civics consisted chiefly of a formal study of the constitution and machinery of the government. The two decades from about 1890 to 1910 mark a trasitional period in the teaching of Civics, which changed the subject from a monotonous study, emphasizing the machinery of government, to a vital subject including the purposes and functions of the government and the relationship of the pupils to his government and to other social agencies. Today Civics holds an important place in the curriculum of secondary school.

The outstanding purpose of instruction in Civics is to produce better citizens and to did pupils in the formation of a higher type of civic character. For the achievement of this objective, the pupils should receive a well-grounded knowledge of the machinery and functions of all the various governmental agencies—local, state and federal. Such knowledge is absolutely necessary for a young citizen to understand and to use later when he participators effectively in government: In addition to this, civic ideals, attitudes, and habits that will operate in the lives of the pupils are important. It encourages an independent thinking and helps in making impartial judgements in civic affairs on the basis of sufficient data, and not on bias, prejudice and or emotion.

Economics

Economics is the science of wealth. It tells us about production, distribution, consumption and exchange of goods and services and deals with human wants and their satisfaction. Human wants are limited. But Economics deals with the satisfaction of human wants with the limited resources available at our disposal.

Early Economic theory sums to have had its origin in Greece, as may be evidenced in the writings of Plato and Aristotle. The word "Economics" comes from the Greek which means household management. Robbins defines Economics as a science that studies human behaviour as a relationship between ends and scarce means which have alternative uses.

Economics did not came into its own as a distinct and separate body of knowledge until the eighteenth century. The impetus to the study of the subject was given by the physiocrats, led by Quesnay, Turgot and others. The work of Adam Smith, Father of the Classical English School of Economic Thought, broadened the views of physiocrats. But in those days, Economics was chiefly concerned with the wealth and power of the nation, but not the welfare of the masses. It was in a formal manner as a logically organized science and was little suited to the needs, abilities and capabilities of pupils.

The nineteenth century saw changes in economic thought that aimed at the well-being of the masses. Beginning about the middle of the century, the movement developed through the writings of Karl Marx and others. The real social implications of Economics were perceived. As was the case with Civics, the last decade of the nineteenth century and the opening decade of the twentieth century marked a transitional period in the form and content of courses in Economics. During this period, textbooks became increasingly concrete and practical, and courses were better adopted to the needs, maturity, and capacities of pupils.

The aim of new Economics is to train pupils in economic citizenship. It plans to aid the pupil in acquiring a knowledge and understanding of the fundamental principles of our economic life so that he may be able to adapt himself intelligently to this phase of his environment and face with understanding and ability the problems that arise. It is evident that the complexity of modern industrial, economic and social life in our country requires that each individual be trained at least in the fundamental principles of everyday economics. In secondary school stage, the subject provides the child with the economic principles and problems relating to present day life , an understanding of economic relationships and the recognition of the social nature of economic activity which will enable to achieve the aim of training pupils in economic citizenship.

By having all the above subjects Social Studies became a complex field, that intended to study human affairs in the social situation. The various branches of study described above are very much inter-related, one cannot develop independently of others. They all begin with man's social life as the foundation of their studies, but they study man's life from different aspects. We may regard them as looking at the same object from different angles. A well-integrated program of Social Studies in the schools, in coordination with other subjects, is essential in order to provide an efficient basis for training boys and girls to become effective citizens.

AIMS AND OBJECTIVES OF SOCIAL STUDIES

The main idea in setting up of aims and objectives is to make the teacher aware of the values to be attained so that they are able to plan teaching programme to select significant and meaningful content to choose suitable teaching methods and techniques and to use appropriate devices for teaching. True, the aims may be idealistic, remote and difficult, but they are not useless. In this connection, Wesley has rightly remarked that "the star is useful though the mariner never reaches". Infact, aims are a true compass to make our journey in the pedagogical sea safe and secure. Speaking more elaborately, they help us in knowing the scope of the subject and the standard of that grade. In short, they are the crux and key of the entire process of teaching and learning.

The aims and objectives of secondary are primarily concerned with the needs of the individual and the society.

So as to obey the general aims and objectives of education, every subject and activity in the school should contribute to those aims and objectives. So, naturally, the aims and objectives of Social Studies will have to be in consonance with the broader aims of education here and now. In this connection John V. Michalls has rightly remarked that "the central of Social Studies is identical with those of general aims and objectives of education."

The Kothari Commission, which has appointed by the Government of Indian in 1964 to advise the government on the national pattern of education and on the general principles and policies of the development of education at all stages and in all aspects, gives the following as the aims of teaching Social Studies in an Indian School: "The aim of teaching Social Studies is to help the students to acquire knowledge of their environment and understanding of human relationships and certain attitudes and values which are Vital for intelligent participation in the affairs of the community, the state, the nation and the world."

Besides these, some other aims and objectives are identified as explained below—

1) "To acquaint the child with his past and present geographical and social environment".

   Social Studies, with its past as well as present knowiedge, provide the child with their geographical and social conditions and the interaction between the two. Not only this, it also compares the present conditions with the past. It gives a clear picture of their surroundings to the prospective citizens.

2) "To enable children to appreciate India's rich cultural heritage."

   The knowledge of Social Studies will help the students in gaining acquaintance with their glorious culture so that they turn as the torch bearers of the inherited culture.

3) "To enable to recognize and get rid of what is undesirable and antiquated, especially in the context of social change."

   A proper content of Social Studies enables the students to recognize the narrow parochial, chauvinistic and obscurantist tendencies and their roots that throw a serious challenge to national integration. This knowledge keeps the students away from these evils.

4) "To build social competence."

Social Studies encourage social competence with co-operation rather rivalry, which is important for the national development.

5) "To build intelligent democratic citizenship."

Social Studies education helps the student to inculcate the values of democracy and acquaint them with their duties that are to be shouldered by them and the rights, which they have to enjoy in this democratic country. Therefore, Social Studies prepares an affective citizenship by making them conscious of their rights and by making them aware of their responsibilities so as to perform their duties properly.

6) "To help the child acquire the right attitudes, knowledge, understanding and competence which we will need in the interaction with social and physical environment."

Social Studies enables the child to understand the process of interaction between physical and social conditions, which will help them in the fulfilment of their basic needs.

7) "To help the child gain insights into spiritual, economic and political values in human behaviour and humans relationships."

An effective programme of Social Studies will help the child in gaining insights into many values, which act as valuable forces in understanding human behaviour and relationship.

8) "To provide a pattern and experience of study that will serve as a foundation for later specializations."

By having diversified areas like History, Geography, Civics, Economics, etc., Social Studies will help the Youngsters in gaining basic knowledge of various fields. So that, it will help them in selecting a particular discipline later in their life.

9) "To develop desirable qualities for an all-round development of a rich personality."

A proper content of Social Studies inculcates the spirit of co-operation, the development of tolerance and an understanding and sympathy for mankind, as well as practice in constructive thinking, reasoning, critical judgement and desirable qualities.

10) "To enable the pupils to use their leisure properly."

One of the important aims of Social Studies is to help the child to use their leisure time effectively. Social Studies provides number of opportunities to show their creativity and provides enough encouragement to develop their interest in making use of leisure time profitably. A happy man in his leisure is usually a happy man in his work. So Social Studies should enable the students to feel at ease by paving the way to spend the leisure time in an effective and happiest way.

11 "To interpret the past as a background for improving the future."

Social Studies lays the foundation of problem-solving nature by depicting the problems of the past and the way in which they are solved. One can easily develop the super-structure by imparting the past. So, it helps the child in viewing a better future by resolving the contemporary social and individual problems based on the past events.

12 "To faster national feelings."

Social Studies develops a national feeling which is necessary to bring national integration and to develop a concept of universal brotherhood.

The above discussion thus for has been concerned chiefly with the general aims of Social Studies. But along with those general aims there are specific aims for each grade or class. Which are inconsonance with the broad aims of Social Studies. At each grade, there are same specific aims that are to be attained at that level. Broadly, the schooling was divided into two stages *viz.*, primary school stage and secondary school stage. Let us see the aims of teaching Social Studies at each level.

Aims of Teaching Social Studies at Primary Level

1. To help the child to explore and understand his social and cultural environment.
2. To develop in the child a sense of belongingness towards the society through gradual widening of his mental horizon from his home and school to the wide world.
3. To acquaint the child with the world of work and to develop in him respect for human labour.
4. To encourage the child to understand that we are striving to build a better life for all.
5. To impress on the child's mind, as he grows, that ours is a rich and composite culture in the formation of which people of different faiths, religions and linguistic groups have made valuable contributions.
6. To develop among children respect for all religions and their places and ways of worship.
7. To encourage the child to understand that we all are equal irrespective of sex, creed, language, etc., and that these are no superior or inferior people and that we all co-operate and organize ourselves to solve our problems.
8. To impress on the child that India, in keeping with the cultural heritage, is one of the important countries of the world that is active in promoting peace, understanding and co-operation among the nations of the world.

Aims of Teaching Social Studies at Secondary Level

In the secondary stage, the field of Social Studies consists of various subjects like Geography, History, Civics, and Economics, so as to provide a background for understanding the present trends. The specific aims of each subjects should be in harmony with the broader aims of Social Studies. Let us see the specific aims of each subject.

History

1. To promote an understanding of the processes of change and development through which human societies have evolved to their present stage of development.

2. To promote an understanding of the common roots of human civilization and an appreciation of the basic unity of mankind.
3. To develop an appreciation of the contributions made by various cultures to the total heritage of mankind.
4. To foster the understanding that the mutual interaction of various cultures has been an important factor in the progress of mankind.
5. To facilitate the study of the history of specific countries in relation to and as part of the general history of mankind.

Geography

1. To gain an understanding of man and his environment.
2. To help students identify the varieties in the distribution of physical and economical phenomena over the surface of the earth, that are associated and give a distinctive character to particular parts of the earth's surface.
3. To help students analyze the ways of life of the people all over the world, their problems in the light of their varying environments and their stages of economic and technical development
4. To develop an appreciation of interdependence of various geographical regions.
5. To help students make generalisation with the help of geographical concepts, the knowledge of which is of great value in understanding, evaluating and reaching decisions about world problems.

Civics

1. To promote active and intelligent citizens who have the necessary civic competence to participate in the community affairs effectively.
2. To develop an intelligent understanding of the structure and working of the civic and political institutions of India.
3. To help the students appreciate the role of the United Nations and Indian's contribution towards maintenance of world peace.

4. To respect each person with regard to his race, colour, creed or sex.

Economics

1. To appreciate the importance of economic systems.
2. To understand the causes of inflation and deflationary gap.
3. To train the students in economic citizenship.
4. To aid the students in acquiring a knowledge and understanding of the fundamental principles of our economic life.
5. To understand the inter-relationship between the economic principles and the problems that are confronted in our day to day life.

Specific Objectives of Social Studies

In order to accomplish the said aims, certain specific objectives must be set up and achieved.

The specific objectives of Social Studies can be said as understanding, acquiring knowledge, developing right type of attitudes, formation of habits and skills.

The basic purpose of Social Studies programme is to provide the motivation, understanding, knowledge and skills necessary for informed and active citizenship. Ideally, each pupil who completes the programme should be motivated to support these principles actively as a patriotic, participating citizen. The selection of the Social Studies materials for inclusion in the school curriculum is made with this purpose in mind. The Social Studies programme is intended to offer opportunities for each pupil to develop—

1. Knowledge of the physical aspects of the world and how such physical factors as climate and topography affect the lives of people in various regions.
2. Knowledge and understanding of how various groups of people have developed social institutions suited to their needs and how various people have encountered the problems in developing their respective cultures and civilizations.

3. Knowledge and understanding of the historical backgrounds of the Government and institutions developed by the people, and of the social, economic and political problems faced by a country and its people.
4. Understanding of and a loyalty to the principles upon which the Government is based.
5. Understanding of the problems faced by the people in a democratic country.
6. Certain skills, habits and attitudes are essential to good citizenship in a democratic country. Those include the personal skills needed by each individual to make use of the varied sources of information commonly available in the field of Social Science. In addition, skills and attitudes are included which are requisite to life in a society in which each citizen is expected to work co-operatively with others and to assume the proper obligation of citizenship.

WHICH TEACHING METHOD CAN HELP BETTER ?

Methods are the ways and means through which one reach his destiny—the aims and objectives that are set fourth. It is the device that helps the teacher to reach the learner. It is not a mere mechanical instrument for passing on facts and figures. It creates the right reaction and response and improves the values of learning and fosters right attitudes. It is the connections like between the two ends of the educational prgramme. In this connection Secondary Education Commission said that "Any method, good or bad, links up the teacher and his pupils into an organic relationship with constant mutual interaction; it reacts not only on the mind of the students but on their intellectual and emotional equipment, their attitudes and values."

Hence, it is of utmost importance to have a dynamic method of teaching, which determines the success or failure of a teacher to a large extent. The Secondary Education Commission has emphasized the need for right methods of teaching in these words: "Every teacher and educationist of experience knows that even the best curriculum and the most perfect syllabus remains dead unless quickened into life by the right methods of teaching and right kind of teachers. Sometimes even an unsatisfactory and unimaginative syllabus can be made interesting and significant by the gifted teacher who does not focus his mind on the subject matter to be taught or the information to be imparted but on his students, their interest and aptitudes, their reaction and response. He judges the success of his lesson not by the amount of matter covered but by the understanding, appreciation and the efficiency achieved by the students."

The origin of modern teaching methodology may be traced to 'great Didactic' of Johann Amos Comenius of seventeenth century who believed that all instruction should be carefully graded and arranged in a natural order. But it is the Rousseau's 'Emile' (18th century) that laid the foundations of the methodology and became the inspiration of forward looking and progressive educators. Then Pestalozzi in 19th century attempted to psychologies instruction. Froebel and Frederich Herbar followed pestilozzi and developed elaborate systems of education. Froebel himself connected more with "kindergarten method" and Herbart was well known with his famous "Herbartian Steps". Now-a-days, many new methods were develcped. In 20th century importance was given to child-centered methods and emphasis was on the socialization of the child. In Social Studies, even more than any other subject in the school, socialization is necessary.

Many methods have been devised for teaching Social Studies. The teacher must familiarize himself with all of them in order to determine which will be most effective in attaining his aims. The choice of suitable method by a teacher depends upon many factors such as the learner, the nature of the subject and the topic, the facilities available and above all the attitude of the teacher. "There are many roads highways and by-ways, royal roads and narrow lanes, delightful paths and rugged and rough ones, functional and decorative ones which need to be tried for meeting particular needs and situations."

The need for various methods was advocated by various scholars saying that "No single method can be advocated as the best for all situations and with all teachers and pupils. Different lessons or units demand different approaches of teaching. Secondly, they help us in avoiding monotomy. If a teacher uses the same method for every circumstance, it can be very monotonous indeed. Hence, there are different methods of teaching, corresponding to the different aims of teaching Social Studies." Let us discuss some of the synonymic methods which the teacher may use according to the needs of a situation.

Lecture Method

It is the oldest method of teaching, that was given by idealistic philosophy. Lecture method is the method of presenting the word picture of an idea or the method of imparting information through a speech. It is the method of depicting everything in words. "The speaker (teacher) speaks (gives lectures) and the listeners (students) listen." It is a traffic of flow of ideas lays emphasis on presentation of the content.

Today, the lecture method is generally held disrepute in secondary schools, regarding as unpsychological method. Being a teacher-centered method, the students are passive learners and feel monotonous after a while and give little consideration to individual differences.

But, it is a very effective in giving factual information and to relate the current issues with the past. It is economical and saves time so that it helps the teacher to cover all the aspects. It simplifiers the work of the teacher and facilitates the teacher to attend the students whenever and wherever they want. Lecture method can also be used with other methods of teaching. Sometimes, the lecture method is unavoidable in subjects like Social Studies because of its vast content.

Problem Solving Method

Problem solving may be defined as a planned attack upon a difficulty or perplexity for the purpose of finding a solution. It is a method in which a person uses his ability to solve problems which confront him. It is an instructional device whereby the teacher and the pupils attempt in a conscious planned purposeful effort to arrive at an explanation or solution to an educationally significant difficulty.

Here, problem itself is the crux of the problem. It presupposes the existence of a problem in the teaching- learning situation. A problem is a sort of obstruction or difficulty which has to be overcome to reach the goal. This method aims at presenting the knowledge to be learnt in the form of a problem. It begins with a problematic situation and consists of continuous, meaningful, well- integrated activity. The problems are set to in students in a natural way and it is ensured that the students are genuinely interested to solve them.

Problem solving is not merely a method of teaching. It is in fact a method of organization of a subject matter. It is an approach to deal with the subject matter. The researches of Quitten and Hanne reveal that as compared to the chronological and topical treatment, problem approach in Social Sciences is much more useful.

Essentially the problem solving approach to learning in Social Studies is meant for training children in the technique of discovery. It is more than learning the formalized procedures for the solution of problems and more than analytical thinking that characteristically proceeds a step at a time. It is also the development of effectiveness in intuitive thinking. It is learning to utilise conceptually adequate modes of thought. It is learning the art of predictive reasoning of manipulating knowledge to make it fit new tasks. It is, in short, developing a style of problem solving that will serve for most of the difficulties encountered in life. The hypothesis on which it is based is this: By generalising what they have learned about the solving of intellectual problems in Social Studies, children can solve their problems of living efficiently and effectively.

Like other methods, problem solving method also have some drawbacks. It takes too much time such that one cannot pass on to all the problems. Too much use of the method will become monotonous and tedious. It needs a very capable teacher.

Project Method

It is the practical outcome of the pragmatic educational philosophy. It was developed and perfected by William Kilpatric, a student of John Deway.

Project method is a natural, whole hearted, problem solving an purposeful activity carried to completion in a social environment. It is a revolt against the traditional bookish and passive environment of the school where in children as obedient masses are carefully drilled and spoon-fed with unrelated and disconnected facts, water-tight compartments and pigeon-hole time-tables.

In the words of Stevenson "A project is problematic act carried to completion in its natural setting. According to Snedden, "Project is a unit of educative work in which the most prominent feature is some form of positive and concrete environment."

This method is based on the principle of 'learning by doing'. It assumes that knowledge grows by application. Moreover, it is based on the fact that the different branches of knowledge are not separable, though they are studied separately for some superficial convenience. Knowledge is indivisible, and project method is a method in accordance with this natural correlation. It is a method of spontaneous and incidental teaching. As the project progresses, the learner or a group of learners goes on picking up pieces of knowledge that may happen to be relevant, necessary and useful.

Project method is in accordance with the Psychological laws of learning. It provides the most natural conditions of learning, with the result the child remembers the principles learned for a longer time. It is a method of self-direction. Thus, it develops creative minds. It yields satisfaction, joy and pride in the finished product of their labours which provide a spur to further creative work in life. But it is a time consuming process and many a time it does not keep the examination and curriculum in view. Hence, it is not possible to follow in a normal class-room situation.

Heuristic Method

Heuristic method was developed by Prof. Henry Edward Armstrong. The method was first used in the teaching of science but later on it was adopted in teaching of Social Studies. The word 'Heuritic' comes from the Greek word 'heurisco' or 'heuriskein' which means to find out. Hence, the heuristic method is the method in which children find out things for themselves and are placed in the position of discoverers or inventors. The heuristic method is a method of nature as advocated by Rouseau in his 'Emile'.

It is a method by which pupils learn to reason for themselves. The method aims at developing a scientific and critical attitude and spirit in the students. The object of the heuristic method in the words of an ancient educationist, "to make pupil more exact, more truthful, observant, thoughtful and dexterous, to lay the solid foundation for future self-education and to encourage the growth of a spirit of enquiry and research"

But this method was discarded in secondary schools. As the students are immature, we can not put them in the position of a discover or inventor. Being a very slow method, it is not possible to cover the curriculum in time by using this method. It is practicable only when there are limited number of students and the teacher is resourceful and capable enough.

Source Method

Source method implies using original material and sources in the teaching and learning of Social Studies.

According to source method, pupils are expected to build up historical, political, social and economic accounts with the help of available sources, documents, historical accounts, biographies and inscriptions, coins, travel accounts, religions and secular literature, etc., By providing first hand experiences this method leads to better understanding of the subject. They understand the process through which we have landed the product.

Study of Social Studies in this method will be more real and interesting. It will make the subject more concrete and meaningful. It develops a sense of vividness and reality. It helps the teacher in satisfying the curiosity among the children and train the children in research.

Along with the said merits, it has its own limitations. It is not always possible for the teacher of schools to have easy access to the sources, particularly the original sources. Carrying out the method is too technical and difficult.

Programmed Learning

Programmed instruction has greatly influenced the teaching learning process in recent years all over the world. B. F. Skinner developed this new method, Programmed instruction, based on his theory of learning called 'Operant Conditioning'. But T.C. Thorndike was the first psychologist, whose findings bear direct relevance to programming; it is related with his 'Law of Effect'.

The basic idea of programmed learning is that the most efficient, pleasant and permanent learning takes place when the students proceed through a course by a large number of small, easy-to-take steps.

Programmed instruction is a process of constructing sequences of instructional material in a way that the rate and depth of learning are maximized, understanding is fastened and the motivation of the student is enhanced. The subject matter of the programme is presented by breaking into small steps in a logical sequence. Changes in the steps occur in quality and quantity. The progress of the learner is at his own pace.

Programmed learning was suffering from certain limitations. It was severely criticized as a threat to replacing the teaching. It is a costly process, so that the poor nations can not undertake. And use of programmed instructional material require expert knowledge and training. An average teacher finds it very difficult to make use of this device. It also argued that there is too much emphasis in learning facts and a very little emphasis is on mastery of principles and concepts, and students have also little awareness of other aspects.

Along these methods there are many more methods to teach Social Studies like laboratory method, Assignment method, story telling method, Question answer method, etc. But each method has its own advantages and limitations as well. Some methods are well suited in some circumstances and to some teacher. No single method can be advocated as the best for all situations and with all teachers and pupils.

THE RESEARCH PROBLEM

The questions to be answered by this study are : What is the level of achievement of secondary school pupils? What are the factors contributing for this achievement? How can we improve the status of present achievement level in Social Studies?

Hence, to answer these questions, the research topic is stated as "Achievement in Social Studies at Secondary School Level".

NEED OF THE PRESENT RESEARCH

The Social Studies has assumed an important role in the education of students in our modern secondary school curriculum. It serves as a type of core in the content alignment. The structure of the current Social Studies offerings can furnish much worthwhile knowledge in realm of secondary school education. It follows that the Social Studies programme in the secondary school curriculum shall be focussed toward the needs of youth and furthering their growth. A major objective of secondary education and Social Studies instruction in the development of an effective citizenship.

The secondary school serves a dual role. It contributes to the development of basic beliefs and skills of citizenship and also promotes the individual's unique abilities. Although both functions contribute ultimately to the same goal, in a better society, they are not always cultivated by the some process or experience and the school must organize its programmes to further both the ends.

There need be no inconsistency, however, between the goal of social education for all students and the development of special social competence among the academically talented. Although the skills of citizenship are essential to all functioning members of a democracy, gifted youth are in a position to exert special influence in society either as leaders or as followers. The Social Studies helps to prepare them for this role by providing learning opportunities that will help tap both their intellectual and leadership potential.

The Social Studies programme is an avenue for fostering attitudes, skills, understandings and competencies that are so essential to effective everyday-living. A purposeful programme must be comprehensive and current in structure to achieve its desired objectives. Constant evaluation is necessary for the improvement of the Social Studies programme.

The objectives of Social Studies education are usually stated in terms of knowledge, understanding, skills, habits and attitudes as illustrated by the following example.

The basic purpose of Social Studies education is to provide the motivation, understanding, knowledge and skills necessary for informed and active citizenship. Ideally, each pupil who completes the Social Studies education should be motivated to support these principles actively as a patriotic, participating citizen. The selection of Social Studies materials for inclusion in the school curriculum is made with this purpose in mind. The Social Studies programme is intended to offer opportunities for each pupil to develop:

1. Knowledge of the physical aspects of the world and how such physical factors as climate and topography affect the lives of people in various regions.
2. Knowledge and understanding of how various groups of people have developed social institutions suited to their needs and how they encountered in developing their responsibilities, cultures and civilizations.
3. Knowledge and understanding of the historical backgrounds of the government and institutions developed by the people and of the social, economic and political problems faced by the country and its people.
4. Understanding of and a loyalty to the principles upon which the government is based.
5. Understanding of the problems faced by all the citizens of a nation.
6. Certain skills, habits and attitudes essential to good citizenship in a democratic republic. These include the personal skills needed by each individual to make use of the varied sources of information commonly available in the social science areas. In addition, skills and attitudes are included which are requisites of life in a society and which each citizen is expected to work co-operatively with others and to assure the proper obligations of citizenship.

Considering the importance, as explained, the achievement of secondary school pupils in Social Studies was taken into consideration for a detailed research study. The results of this study will help in bringing out the remedial measures for the failures of an unreasonable quantity every years.

STUDY OBJECTIVES

The following objectives are to be achieved by this study.

1. To find out the level of achievement in Social Studies of secondary school pupils.
2. To compare the achievement in Social Studies of secondary school boys and girls.
3. To compare the achievement in Social Studies of the pupils studying in private and government secondary schools.
4. To compare the achievement in Social Studies of secondary school pupils residing in rural and urban areas.

SCOPE AND LIMITATIONS

Social Studies is one of the compulsory subjects at secondary school level. It prepares good citizens besides fulfilling many aims and objectives of education. Considering the role of Social Studies education in human living, the present study is limited to the study of achievement in Social Studies. Importance was given to sex, locale of the school and type of management. The other factors which promote or deteriorate the Social Studies achievement at secondary school level were not taken into consideration due to the dearth of manual, material and time resources.

2

RELATED RESEARCH

Any worthwhile research study in any field of knowledge requires an adequate familiarity with the work which has already been done in the same area. A summary of the writings of recognized authorities and of previous research provides evidence that the research is familiar with what is already known and what is still unknown and untested. Since effective research is based upon past knowledge, this step helps to eliminate the duplication of what has been already done. It is a valuable guide to define the problem, to recognize its significance, to suggest promising data and gathering devices, to appropriate study design, to identify sources of data, to make effective analysis and to arrive at fruitful conclusions.

Citing studies that show substantial agreement and those that seem to present conflicting conclusions helps to sharpen and define understanding of existing knowledge in the problem area, provides a background for the research issue. Parading a long list of annotated studies relating to the problem is ineffective and inappropriate. Only those studies that are plainly relevant, competently excecuted, and clearly reported should be considered.

In searching related literature, the researcher should note certain important. They include **1**. Reports of closely related studies that have been investigated, **2**. Design of the study, including procedures employed and data-gathering instruments used, **3**. Populations that were sampled and sampling methods employed, **4**. Variables that were defined, **5**. Extraneous variables that could have affected and findings, **6**. Faults that could have been avoided, and **7**. Recommendations for further research.

Reviews of expert researchers can be useful in providing helpful idea and suggestions. Though the review articles which summarize related studies are useful, they do not provide a satisfactory substitute for an independent work, it is the first steps in the research process. It is a valuable guide to define the problem, to recognise its significance, to suggest promising data-gathering devices, to appropriate study design and sources of data for effective analysis and to arrive at fruitful conclusions.

The search for related literature is a time consuming process, even then, it is necessary for a good research work. Hence, this chapter is meant for the study of reasons which contributed to the immediate investigation on the achievement of social studies.

Education plays a vital role in building a society. A modern society can not achieve its aims of economic growth, technical development and cultural advancement without fully harnessing the talents of its citizens. Educationists, thus, strive to develop fully the intellectual potentialities of the students and make efforts to see that their potentialities are fully realized and channelized for the benefit of the individuals and of the society.

Educational opportunities, though open to all, do not seem to engage to any reasonable extent the capacities of those who seek to avail themselves of them. An eternal question baffling parents, educators and national planners is: Why do students of demonstrated ability flop in their academic efforts at school or college examinations? Academic underachievement, more than academic failure, constitutes a grave problem as it amounts to wastage of human resources which is construed as an irreparable loss to the society, which a developing country like ours can ill-afford. This stimulated a number of researchers to undertake studies, like the present study, on factors influencing achievement; a review of which is presented here under.

There are a number of researches on achievement and the factors that are influencing the achievement of students. Achievement is influenced by many factors like values, intelligence, creativity, socio-economic status, the level of aspiration, etc., and the views of various researchers on different factors are cited here under.

Taylor (1964) stated that the value, the student places upon his own worth, effects his academic achievement. Very low level of expectation tends to make a pupil accept very low standard of achievement, very high expectations lead to discouragement and diminished effort because he feels he cannot live up to what is required of him. To be practical, the level of expectation needs to be general to suit to each individuals capability.

Acharyulu (1978) while studying interactive effects creativity on achievement found that intelligence has positive effect on academic achievement. We also found that along with intelligence, creativity also has positive effect. Menon, P.N.(1980) has also found the same results. This was in agreement with the result of Vijayalkshmi (1980).

The study of Singh (1982) again showed that verbal, non-verbal, and total creative thinking variables had positive and significant relationship with academic achievement of high school boys and girls. This was strengthened by the studies of Makhija (1970). He finds that intelligence had a significantly positive influence on scholastic achievement.

Another investigator, Zachria (1977), also attempted to find out the effect of attitude and interest on the achievement in Social Studies of pupils of tenth grade. He found that there was a positive correlation between the secondary school pupils achievement in Social Studies and their attitude. The pupil's interest in Social Studies was closely related to their achievement in the subject at all levels.

Zacharia also found that the pupils intelligence was a major factor in influencing their achievement in Social Studies and observed that pupils' attitude and intelligence scores were more or less equally correlated with their achievement in Social Studies. But pupils' intelligence was not a prominent factor in influencing their attitude and interest in Social Studies.

The study of George (1966) revealed that the pupils with high intelligence were identified as better adjusted and higher achievers in all the groups studied.

The longitudinal study by Reddy (1978) found academic adjustment significantly related to scholastic performance. Among other results, it is of significance to note that the attitude to self, learning, achievement, parents, teachers and peers were found to be positively related to academic adjustment and scholastic performance.

Soman (1977) investigated the overlap of fourteen affective variables belonging to basic personality dimensions of achievement in mathematics. The study revealed that personal adjustment variables and anxiety variables had a considerable influence on achievement in mathematics. The dominant personality factor identified for the over-achievers was individual adjustment factor.

Students' home, health, social and emotional adjustment, students' study habits and their attitude towards education figured as some of the non-intellectual correlates of academic achievement in a study by Chopra (1988). The study showed that academic achievement had a positive relationship with attitude towards education and also with the study habits of students. Further, home adjustment was found to be more closely related to academic, than emotional, health, and social adjustment.

In the study of Pyari (1980) the relationship between family attachment scores and educational achievement scores was found to be negatively significant. Theoretical, aesthetic, social and religious values were positively and significantly related with educational achievement, while economic and political values were negatively and significantly related.

Socio-economic status has also its impact on achievement of children, especially in Indian context, since it consists of different classes as elsewhere. So it is natural for the researchers to think of the extent to which home conditions influence the scholastic achievement of children.

Satyanandam (1969) highlighted two sub-aspects of socio economic status, namely, educational level of parents and economic status of parents. According to the researcher, the children of graduate parents performed far better than the children of matriculate parents. Children of upper and lower, and upper and middle economic strata only differed significantly on the variable of academic affairs.

Chatterji, et al. (1971) investigated the effect of parents' education, family size and general condition of the home upon scholastic achievement. And they find out that the economic conditions of the family have no effect upon the scholastic achievement in all the intellectual ability groups. Similarly, possession of a study- room had no favourable effect in increasing the achievement score in almost all the cases. The family size and the number of siblings were inversely related to the scholastic achievement specially in the low intellectual level. Parents' help has significant positive contribution towards higher achievement. And parents' educational level was directly related to the achievement of their children. But fathers' occupation didn't show considerable effect. However, the study conclusively demonstrated parents' education as related to scholastic achievement. This argument was strengthened by the studies of Khanna (1980) by establishing a significant and positive relationship between socio-economic status (SES) and academic achievement. But SES was found unrelated to academic achievement in the studies of Salunke (1979). Even though he found that educational facilities and emotional happiness in home contributed positively to the pupils' performance.

One or other personality traits have time and again been found to be conducive to success in academic field. But it is of great concern to find out how they influence academic achievement an in what way. Many studies were conducted to probe into the relationship of contain personality variables with achievement.

Siddiquir (1979), while studying the effects of achievement motivation and personality on academic achievement, found that there was a mutual relationship between intelligence, achievement and personality. And personality has a positive correlation with achievement motivation.

Singh and Kumar (1977) and Bhushan and Ahuja (1977), while inquiring into the relationship of anxiety and achievement, came to the same conclusion - anxiety to have a negative relationship with achievement. But contrary to this, Ravinder (1977) revealed that general anxiety by itself had little effect on academic achievement and that combination of anxiety with intelligence considerably increased the accuracy of predicting academic performance. Yet, in another study, Hussain (1977) gave the conclusion that anxiety was found to bear a curvilinear relationship with academic achievement.

Though self-concept has been studied as one of the many variables in a number of investigations, Shah (1978) and Goswami (1978) studied it as a major variable and looked into its relationship with achievement. He has given the conclusion that the relationship between self-concept and academic achievement was significantly positive and linear. In agreement with this conclusion Goswami (1978) added that the rural students tended to have a good self-concept that the urban ones. Another study which also yielded a similar conclusion was that of Sharma (1979).

It is of extreme important to educators in general and teachers in particular, to know why some students achieve high while others achieve low in the same school environment? Are there any inherent characteristics in students which play a role in this discrimination? There has been a continuous research in this area to delve into greater depths of the problem.

Jain (1978) found that bright achievers were characterized by better study habits and higher achievement motivation than dull achievers.

Agarwal (1975), who made psycho-social study of academic under-achievement concluded that under-achievers were comparatively less emotionally mature, less calm, less placid, less prone to getting into difficulties, less able to face reality, and possessing less ego strength than over-achievers. On comparison of values, over-achievers had stranger educational, social and humanistic values than under-achievers.

The studies, conducted by Nagpal (1979), Saun (1980), and Patel and Joshi (1977) revealed the same result that the under-achievers have social, adjustment, emotional etc., problems in comparison to over-achievers. In Nagpal's study, the underachievers reported a greater number of adjustment problems and more academic adjustment problems. Same conclusions were drawn from the study of Saun. The high achievers were well adjusted with family and were also better adjusted personality than the under-achievers. A variety of conclusions were drown in the study of Ghuman (1976). It shown that over-achievers and under-achievers did not differ significantly on any of the variables, namely, aptitudes, achievement motivation or personality traits. The study attributed over-achievement primarily to non-intellective personality variables, and under-achievement to intellective factors.

Of late, researchers have been trying to identify what types of variables interacting in the environment of a school affect the academic achievement of students and to what extent.

Taking into consideration the climate in the institution as one of the variables in the study, and working on a sample of scheduled caste students, Rani (1980) Shashidhar (1981) concluded that academic achievement was influenced, among other things, by institutional factors. Desai (1979) and Hirunval (1980) both found a positive relationship between class room climate and pupil's academic achievement. Further more, an increase in school condition was likely to lead to better achievement. (Subramanyam, 1981). In, yet, another study Srinivasa Rao and Subrahmanyam (1982) reported similar results.

All these studies highlightened the importance of environment provided by the school itself in the promotion of better achievement.

Aspiration is a natural phenomenon of human life, and educational aspiration is no exception. Level of aspiration was also considered to play a significant role in scholastic achievement.

Menon (1972) found that job aspiration, educational aspiration and general ambition were strongly associated with high achievement, particularly in girls. Ram Kumar (1972) observed a strong association between achievement and goal discrepancy. Agreeing with these results Kuppuswami (1974) informed that the achievement in school is closely related to the level of aspiration.

In contrary, studies of Gould and Koplan (1940) Sears (1940), Holt (1942), Schultz and Recciuti (1954) found no relationship between scholastic achievement and level of aspiration. Sharma (1979) also found that the level of aspiration did not influence academic achievement.

But the studies of Shukla (1973) revealed that the level of aspiration determines the limits of academic achievement to some extent only.

De (1979) found that body were superior to girls in general scholastic ability in geography.

Godgil made an investigation into the causes of failures in Social Sciences in the public examination at the end of standard X conducted by the S.S.C.E. Board, Pune, in March, 1968. The main conclusions drawn from the study were; failures in Social Sciences were due to the inadequacies in grading the subject, in mastering the subject by teachers, in guidance in writing answers, and unsatisfactory translations of the question papers from English into other languages. Another factor is poor equipment in the schools, which creeps into the results. Another reason he find out for large scale failures was due to lack of required percentage of qualified teachers to teach Social Sciences.

Achievement in Social Studies was not hindered because of medium of instruction (Mishra, et al., 1973). But it was not in conformity with the results of Anand (1973).

Pandey (1974) found that achievement in Social Studies was in effect with the background from which the students come. The industrial background was more favourable for high academic achievement than rural background. But in the study of Patel (1977) it was observed that there was no significant difference in achievement between urban boys and urban girls, but in case of rural areas, girls were superior to boys, and he added, that there is a direct relationship between achievement in history and geography and age.

A study by Fernandaz, Massey, and Dornburch (1976) revealed that the Social Studies enjoy an esteem among students, that, at the best, could be described as modest. Students were found to believe that competence in their Social Studies was much less important for success in their future occupational roles than competence in their other subjects. This view was reinforced by similar beliefs on the part of parents, counselors and friends. The investigators noted that because students viewed Social Studies classes as unimportant, they were unwilling to expand a great deal of effort on their studies in this area. Further, there was a wide spread belief among students that if they did 'poor work' in their Social Studies classes they still would receive an acceptable high grade. The investigators concluded that students' tendencies to view Social Studies instruction as unimportant and academically soft were rooted (1) in students' lack of specific understanding of the knowledge and skills central to the Social Studies, and (2) in students' failure to see any personal benefit deriving from lessons in Social Studies.

The above findings show that the problem of achievement, especially in Social Studies, attracted considerable attention and that there were so many angles to study this problem. The topic still considered to be important from the point of social utility, and on a very large number of students were showing under-achievement in their social studies, even in case of top scorers.

3

RESEARCH DESIGN

Research design is a framework for research problem. Research design is the plan, structure, and strategy of investigation conceived so as to obtain answers to research questions (Kerlinger). It is a process of deliberate anticipation dedicated towards bringing out an unexpected situation under control.

Designing is regarded as the heart of the study, because it is that part of the study which decides the fate of the research. It is upon the design that the nature of data to be collected will very much a depend. And it helps in collecting and analysing data in an economic, efficient and relevant manner. Therefore, it is desirable to have a methodologically well designed research plan.

In the present chapter, the following three aspects which are concerned with the design of the present study have been discussed in detail.

The research procedure includes the operational definitions of the different terms used in the study, the geographical area, hypotheses that were formulated for the study and the rational of these hypotheses.

The selection of sample includes the sampling techniques used, reasons for the selection of a particular sampling technique, and the selection of sample according to different variables.

The selection of tool includes the selection of suitable tool for collection of data, description of the tool selected, testing its suitability for the present study, and the procedures followed in administering the tool to collect the data required for the present study.

Taking objectives into consideration the following three variables were selected for the study - 1. Boys versus Girls, 2. Urban students versus Rural Students, and 3. Private versus Government school students.

After deciding the objectives and variables, the tool to be used for the collection of data was finalised. So as to study the achievement in Social Studies, marks of the students in their Social Studies public examination were taken into consideration.

The population for the present study consists of X class students, who have Social Studies as one of the subjects. After a detailed study of the different techniques of sampling, the stratified sampling technique is found to be the most suitable one and so that it was used for the collection of data. A sample of six hundred students were selected through this stratified sampling technique by taking the different variables under study into consideration.

Before going into the details of the above said aspects it is worthwhile to discuss the operational definitions of the key terms used in the present study which will enlighten the characteristics involved in each term.

OPERATIONAL DEFINITIONS OF KEY TERMS

The operational definitions of the important terms that were used in the present study are discussed and defined herewith.

Social Studies

The very name of Social Studies itself reveals the meaning of the term. The word 'social' refers to society and 'studies' implies areas to be learn. . Thus, Social Studies denotes that it is an area of study which is concerned with the knowledge of society, that is social aspects.

Social Studies is the scientific study of human society and social relationship.

Peter H. Martorella has observed the Social Studies as "It is more accurate to think of Social Studies as an applied field which attempts to fuse scientific knowledge with ethical, philosophical, religious and social considerations which arise in the process of decision-making as practiced by citizens."

The Secondary Education Commission in India, 1952-53, stated Social Studies as "a complex subject having a group of studies and whose object is to adjust the students to their social environment which includes the family, community, state and nation".

The Social Studies Committee of Schools Board, Victoria (U.S.A) in its publication, Social Studies for Schools, has described Social Studies as "what we study in Social Studies is the life of man in some particular place, at particular time".

According to James High, "The Social Studies are the school mirrors of the scholarly findings of the social sciences. Such data as social scientists may gather is integrated and simplified to appropriate levels of experience for children an all the grades".

John V. Michaelis states that "the Social Studies are concerned with man and his social and physical environment, they deal with human relationships.

James Hammings defined Social Studies as "A study of relations and inter-relations-historical, geographical and social".

According to J.M. Forester, "Social Studies, as the very name suggests, is the study of society and its chief aim is to help pupils to understand the world in which they have to live".

The Secondary Education commission of the National Education Association (USA) has defined Social Studies in these words, "Social Studies are understood to be those subjects, whose matter relates directly to the organisation and development of human society and to man as a member of social group".

According to Griffin, "Social Studies is not an individual subject, discipline or science. It is a field of study which deals with man, his relation with other man and his environment. It draws its content from the several social sciences but its characteristics are not determined by any one of them".

From the above definitions it is evident that the Social Studies is an off-spring of Social Sciences, bearing a variety of areas. It is a complex subject that touches all the aspects of human life, especially the social aspect. It studies the human relations as the pivot theme.

Achievement

Achievement, in an educational institution, may be taken to mean any desirable learning that is observed in the student. Since the word desirable implies a value judgement, it is obvious that a particular learning may be referred to as achievement or otherwise depending on whether it is considered desirable or not. Understood in this way, any behaviour that is learned may come within the scope of achievement. Achievement, according to Smith (1969), and Spencer and Helmrich (1983), is the task-oriented behaviour that allows the individual's performances to be evaluated according to some internally or externally imposed criterion, that involves the individual in competing with others or that otherwise involves some standard of excellence (Morgan, et. al, 1986).

There is no gain saying the fact that learning is not limited to mere acquisition of information, it also includes attitudes, interests, values, etc. Modern personality characteristics of the individual are learned. Therefore, the acquisition of desirable characteristics is as much an achievement as is knowledge of the principles of science of facts, world history or language and literature. Although achievement is used in this broad sense it is customary for schools and colleges to be concerned to a great extent with the development of knowledge, understanding and acquisition of skills (Narayana Rao, 1980). This may be in part owing to the fact that in the intellectual field the teacher can be relatively more certain of achieving the objectives he had set for himself than in other areas or domains.

Academic achievement is related to the acquisition of principles and generalizations and the capacity to perform efficiently certain manipulations of objects, symbols and ideals. Assessment of academic performance has been largely confined to an evaluation in terms of information, knowledge and understanding. It is universally accepted that the acquisition of actual data, is not an end in itself but an individual who has received education should show evidence of having understood them. But for obvious reasons the examinations are largely confined to the measurement of the amount of information which students have acquired.

Achievement in terms of subject matter is conventionally assessed in our institutions by employing a system of marks of grades. It has been strongly argued that marked are necessary for effective teaching-learning. Trabue (1920) felt that for classification, guidance and evidence of effort, marks are necessary. A committee of Principals of California listed the purposes of marks as the indication of the degree of mastery of subject matter and the prediction of future success. Madsen (1930) points out that marks set goals and motivate the students. Symons (1927) listed among the purposes of marks incitement of study, promotion of competition, determination of promotion, assistance in education and vocational guidance, awarding credits and honours. It is universally accepted that marks serve for the basis of classification and certification, motivation and measurement of educational performance.

Achievement Test

Freeman (1965) defines a test of educational achievement as a test designed to measure knowledge, understanding, and skills in a specified subject or group of subjects. Thus, according to him an educational achievement test measures an individual's knowledge and understanding or skills in a particular branch of knowledge. Further, Freeman is of the view that through educational achievement test, it is possible to ascertain how much does a person know after receiving education or training in a particular branch of knowledge. The standardized achievement tests are used to determine the degree of achievement in a specific subject matter (Smith, Krouse and Atkinson, 1969). Achievement test (Best, 1982) attempts to measure what an individual has learned his or her present level of performance.

An achievement test is also used for purposes of guidance and counselling. It has found useful in remedial teaching prgramme as well as in determining the class to which a student should be admitted into. Administration of these tests at regular intervals is helpful to the teachers in knowing the kinds of difficulties faced by the pupil in learning. Finally, it may be stated that the achievement test may be used as an aid in the evaluation of teaching, instructional techniques, and the curriculum.

Private Schools

Private schools, here, mean the schools that were managed by private organisations or persons, either personally or totally, were regarded as private schools. So, the public schools, Government recognized or aided schools managed by individuals or private agencies were included under 'private schools.

Government Schools

The schools under the sole management of Government were included under Government schools. So, the schools managed by Zilla Praja Parishads, Municipalities and Government were included in this category.

Urban Schools

The Schools located in an urban areas were considered urban schools. An urban area should have a municipal corporation, cantonment board or notified town area, etc.; should have a minimum population of five thousands; should have 75% of its male working population engaged in non-agricultural pursuits and should have a population of at east 400 persons per square kilometer.

Rural Schools

The schools located in rural areas were considered rural schools. A rural area should have a population below five thousands, with 75% of its population engaged in agricultural pursuits.

VARIABLES

Choosing the appropriate variables is of utmost important phenomenon on a research so as to achieve the set objectives. Keeping the objectives in view, following three variables were chosen—1. Boys versus Girls 2. Private versus Government schools 3. Rural versus urban schools. The rational for choosing the above stated variables is discussed here under.

Boys versus Girls

In olden days, there was a yawning gulf in the education of boys and girls, especially in the Indian context. The culture-bound Indians kept their female children behind the four walls of the house, whereas the mole children were provided with all educational opportunities. Slowly, the traditions and superstitions started to disappear and the women's education gained importance and many parents are encouraging their daughters to pursue higher education. It was mainly because of the impact of Western civilization and the social reforms, that are carried out by great people like Jawaharlal Nehru, who advocated woman education by saying "If you educate a man, you educate a person; if you educate a woman you educate the entire family". Now, Women are working in almost all fields and they are also showing excellence in all fields. But, there are same variations in between boys and girls in their education. It is because of some natural variations like physiological conditions, exposure to the society, etc. The boys are exposed to the society to a larger extent, but the girls spend most of their time in going through books or helping their parents at home. It is also familiar that girls mature faster than boys at the early adolescent state, both physically and mentally. The above factors will have their own impact on the Social Studies achievement. So, a comparison between boys and girls will reveal any difference that exists in the achievement in Social Studies.

Private Schools versus Government Schools

The reputation of private schools is generally better when compared with that of the government schools. The pupils are exposed to better conditions and better study atmosphere in private schools. If better facilities are not provided in private schools, the parents will question the authorities concerned immediately as they pay higher fees for their children. The library facilities an the use of audio visual aids will play a major role in the achievement of Social Studies. The quality of teaching is also supposed to be better in private schools. The teachers take more interest in teaching in private schools as they are always either in the fear of losing their jobs or immediately being questioned by the managements about the quality of their teaching. And the management also takes care of their quality of teaching as they are always wanted to be best among the other schools. The standard of teaching, therefore, is supposed to be different in private and government schools, and hence the achievement in Social Studies will also be different in these two types of schools. Thus, it is important to study the degree of difference in achievement in these schools.

Rural Schools versus Urban Schools

The urban schools are well equipped in many aspects when compared with the rural schools. The buildings, the libraries, the teaching staff, the educational atmosphere, the competitive spirit among the pupils, the amenities provided to pupils to pursue education, the exposure to the exhibitions and to various historical places, the habits like stamp collection, coin collection, etc., the student participation in teaching learning process, the use of audio-visual aids, etc., will always be better in urban schools than in rural schools. These will play a commendable role in the achievement of Social Studies. A comparison between rural and urban school pupils will bring out the difference in the achievement of Social Studies, if there exists any.

HYPOTHESES

Achievement in Social Studies refers to a tangible accomplishment or proficiency or performance in Social Studies as measured using a test, in Social Studies.

Anyone is assessed and measured in terms of scores or achievement in a particular subject. If one is thorough with the subject along with the required personality characteristics, he will be in a good position to show better achievement in the subject.

The achievement mainly depends on intelligence and aptitude. The other factors that appear to be associated with achievement are curiosity, ability to apply knowledge to new situations, memory, insight into the subject, skills in learning, conducive teaching learning environment, socio-economic status, adjustment, etc. It is of great importance to provide conducive learning atmosphere to the pupils for better achievement.

Social Studies education has become an important prerequisite for any individual to lead a happy and harmonious life in the society, and hence it is made a compulsory subject upto 10+ level.

The following hypotheses to identify the achievement differences in different categories of secondary pupils, have been formulated for the present study.

Hypothesis 1

The secondary school pupils will possess high achievement in Social Studies.

Hypothesis 2

There will be a significant difference in Social Studies achievement between boys and girls of secondary schools.

Hypothesis 3

There will be a significant difference in Social Studies achievement between the pupils of private and government secondary schools.

Hypothesis 4

There will be a significant difference in Social Studies achievement between the pupils of rural and urban secondary schools.

SAMPLE

After finalizing the variables of the present study, three important things were considered, namely, 1. What will be the scope of the study?, 2. What will be the population or universe? and 3. The most important aspect is to decide whether the entire population concerned with the subject has to be covered or a small group out of the population is to be selected as representative of the whole population. The 'entire population' here refers to all the tenth class student of Guntur district, who are students of Social Studies at tenth class level.

For studying a social problem, it is difficult to study the whole universe of the problem under study. Selection of a group as a representative of the population, hence was found to be more convenient and suitable. This technique leads to a considerable saving of time , effort and finance. When the number of students selected is small, it is possible to make a detailed and intensive study. This generally leads to more accurate and reliable results. As this sampling technique has many advantages, it was selected for the collection of the data. But the sample must be picked up in a manner that it represents the universe as a whole.

In any social research, various methods are used for selection and drawing of samples. After a detailed study of all these methods and considering the variables selected for the research work, the stratified sampling method was considered most suitable.

For stratified sampling, firstly the universe has to be divided into smaller homogenous groups, in the light of the variables considered. Then from each group, a sample has to be selected. Every sampling unit in the population is placed in one of the groups prior to selection of the sample, so that the sum of the groups is identical with the population.

As a sampling technique it has certain merits and advantages. Stratified sampling is a refinement over simple random sampling since, in addition to randomness, stratification introduces a secondary element of control as a means of increasing precision and representativeness. A stratified sample is, infact, a weighted combination of random sub-samples joined to give an over-all sample value. In this context, Auckoff has said that "stratified sampling enables the researcher to make a comparison of properties of the state as well as to estimate population characteristics."

Stratified sampling method is the ideal one when comparison between different variables has to be made. For example, if comparison has to be made between rural and urban school pupils or between private and government school pupils, it would be very difficult to select the required number of units through any other method of sampling, except stratified sampling method. If any other method is used, the problem of bias and prejudice creeps in.

Replacement of units is also possible in the stratified sampling method. Normally, if a particular unit is not accessible for a study, it is difficult to replace it by another, but in this method it is possible. Stephen stated that "stratification automatically brings out a replacement of persons lost to the sample, by the person of the same stratum, thus partly corrects bias that would result if there were no replacement of loses." As the entire population is divided into particular strata, it is easy and convenient to replace an inaccessible case by an accessible one.

In stratified sampling method, much depends on stratification process. The following precautions are taken while stratifying the population: The variables involved in the study were taken note of; care was taken to see that each stratum in the Universe was large enough in size so that selection of items could be done on random basis; the strata formed were definite and clear cut; each stratum was free from influence of the other.

Certain fundamental principles were considered before actually selecting the sample to make the sample scientific and clear-cut.

Firstly, the universal was clearly defined. In the technical phraseology of research, the whole population out of which the samples are selected is known as the "Universe". For the present research work, the universe includes all the students who were studying tenth class in secondary schools. The study was limited to a particular geographical area viz, Guntur district, to facilitate appropriate sample selection and to avoid bias and prejudice.

Secondly, units are selected keeping the following points in view : 1. ***Clarity:*** The unit should be clearly defined in unambiguous terms. This would make the study easy and efficient. For the present research work, a sample unit was a pupil of tenth class studying in any school of Guntur district; 2. ***Suitability:*** A good unit should be well suited to the problem under study, since the problem is concerned with the achievement in Social Studies of tenth class pupils of Guntur district the unit selected is well suited to the problem. 3. ***Accessibility :*** The unit selected should be easily accessible to the researchers. If the units selected are difficult to reach and if we fail to make use of them, the study would be vitiated. The selected sampling unit, *i.e.*, a tenth class pupil is easily accessible since he/she could be approached in any secondary school.

Thirdly, a source list must be obtained or prepared. A source list which contains the names of the units of the universe from which the sample may be selected. It may exist even before the beginning of the project or it may be prepared afresh by the investigators themselves. A source list was prepared consulting the district education authorities to select the sample.

Besides considering these principles, it is extremely important to think about. The size of the sample to the sample to be selected. If the sample is either too small or too large, it well make the study difficult and also make the results untenable. According to Parten, an optimum sample in a survey is one which fulfills the requirements of effective representativeness, reliability and flexibility. The size of the sample for the present research work was decided after considering the following factors.

Since an intensive study was planned, a very large number of samples were not selected. In case of an intensive study, a very large number of samples are not so useful as they involve huge consumption of the resources. Hence, a reasonably smaller sample was found convenient.

The size and selection of the sample will also be influenced by the nature of the universe. If the universe is homogenous, even small-sized sample may yield dependable and required results. If the universe is heterogeneous, small-sized samples will not be useful. In case of this study, the heterogeneous universe was split into smaller homogenous strata, and the samples were selected from these strata. For example, all the tenth class pupils of Guntur district were broadly grouped under rural and urban pupils. A required number of sample was selected from each of these two groups.

The investigators need to determine the number of the groups to be formed. In case the number of groups proposed is large, the size of the samples shall have to be large so that every group should be of proper size and suit to the requirements of the study. In case the number of groups proposed is small, even small-sized samples can fulfil the requirements. In the case of the present study, the number of groups into which the universe was divided are-girls and boys, private and government, and rural and urban schools. Since the number of groups are move, a reasonably large sample was to be selected from each of these groups.

Practical considerations and accuracy also play a vital role in determining the size of the sample. Every study is guided by certain practical considerations such as time, resources, accessibility of the data, etc. Generally, it is believed that a large-sized sample generally produces accurate results. This, of course, depends upon the sampling technique used. If the sampling technique is scientific, even small-sized samples can produce dependable and accurate results. While selecting the size of the sample for the present study, practical considerations like the availability of resources and time were taken into consideration. Care was taken to make the sample selection techniques as scientific as possible.

The size of the sample is also governed by the size of the tools to be used. In case the tools are short, and the questions asked pertain to certain limited factors, a large sample can be selected. In case the tools are large and the questions are complicated, the sample should be small in size. So that, from administrative point of view, the investigators may not be put to necessary troubles. In the present study, a reasonably large sample was selected as the investigators used the marks of the sample.

The sampling method also determines the size of the sample. When random sampling is used, the samples have to be large. On the other hand, if samples are selected through stratified sampling method, the reliability can be achieved even with the help of small-sized samples.

After taking all these factors, which influence the sample, into consideration , it was decided that an ideal sample would consist of three hundred pupils. This sample is small enough to avoid intolerable sampling errors and large enough to get accurate results.

Taking the variables which compare rural and urban areas at first instance, the universe which geographically consisted of Guntur district was split into rural and urban areas. An equal number of sample was taken from both rural and from urban secondary schools, that is, 150 pupils from rural and 150 from urban schools.

The sample from the rural areas had to be selected from the tenth class pupils of Zilla Praja Parishad high schools and private high schools. To select the sample from the private high schools and Zilla Praja Parishad high schools of rural areas, the lottery method as suggested by Best was used. In this method the names of all private high schools were written on slips of equal size, the slips were folded round, mixed well and kept in a container. It was decided to select three schools from private school. So three paper slips were picked up from the container and the schools were thus chosen for sampling. Twenty five tenth class pupils were taken as sample from each of the three private high schools given equal importance to both boys and girls. The same lottery method was used for ZPP schools and Selected sample from them.

Thus, a total sample of 150 were chosen from rural schools. Out of these 75 were boys and 75 were girls; 75 were from private high schools and 75 were from Government high schools.

Table 1 : Sample Distribution in Rural Schools

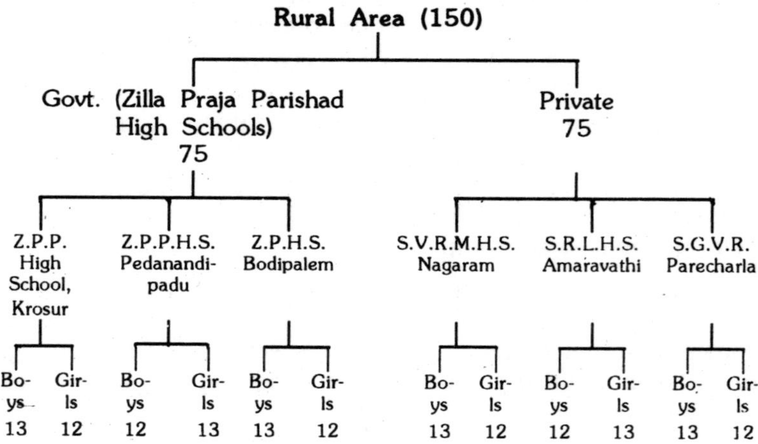

The sample of urban area was selected from the Guntur town. A source list of all high schools present in this town was prepared. After the preparation of the source list of high schools, it was divided into government and private schools. Equal number of private and government schools *i.e.*, three schools from each category was selected. Further, equal number of boys and girls from each sub-sample was selected. For selecting the different categories of samples and sub-samples of urban area, the lottery method as explained in the case of rural sampling was applied.

Table 2 : Sample Distribution in Urban Schools

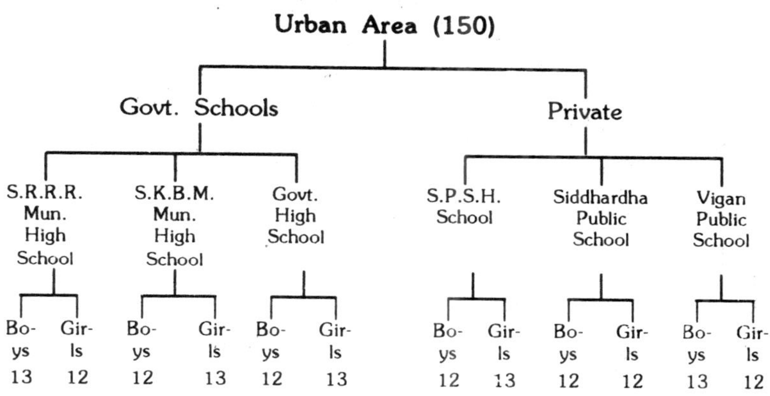

The total sample includes: Rural schools—150 and Urban Schools—150, Girls—150 and Boys—150; Urban schools—150 Private schools—150. The total sample was 300 tenth class pupils studying in secondary schools.

DATA COLLECTION

A research tool plays a major role in any worthwhile research as it is the sole factor in determining the sound data and in arriving at perfect conclusions about the problem for study in hand which ultimately helps in providing suitable remedial measures to the problem concerned. A researcher in the process of data collection requires various types of techniques and tools, which may vary in their complexity, design, administration and interpretation. Each tool is appropriate for the collection of certain types of information for researcher's investigation and for testing hypotheses. The researcher may select one of the available tools or techniques which will suit his purpose and provide most appropriate information for his investigation. On the other hand, when the researcher feels that the existing research tools do not serve the purpose, he can construct his own.

Hence, there are two ways to the selection and use of tools. The first one is construction of the tools independently by the researcher. Many problems are involved in this style. As cautioned by Anand and Padma, "A note of caution has to be struck when a researcher develops a tool for his study by merely polling some items and does not subject it to the sophisticated techniques of tool construction. The result would be the obvious, a poor quality research".

The above statement reveals that the preparation and standardization of a tool is itself a major task and one should take care in aspects like selection of area and samples, polling up of statements related to the area, consulting the experts, and application of sophisticated statistical techniques.

The second type is selection of standardized tools. Hence also it involves a tedious job in locating the tools and in identifying their usefulness to study the problem in hand. Even then this technique is very useful when a research work involves a good number of variables. Some people believe that some of the instruments, that are available, do not measure up to their standards. Hence they go for new ones. In some instances, consideration should be given to the logistics of the situation. Lack of time and financial resources for the construction of a tool, many researchers prefer to follow one among the best available. In these cases, the most logical procedure that one can follow is to choose the best instrument available for the purpose.

To measure the achievement in Social Studies marks of public examination in Social Studies were taken into consideration. It was done so because there was no standardized achievement test to meet the requirements of the present study. The examination was conducted by the Board of the Secondary Education, Government of Andhra Pradesh. The marks will effectively serve the research purpose.

4

DATA ANALYSIS AND FINDINGS

Studying the tabulated material of mass data in order to determine the inherent facts or meanings is referred to as analysis of data. Data analysis involves breaking down the existing complex factors into simpler parts and putting the parts together in new arrangements for purposes of interpretation.

So as to analyse the data from the mass data collected it need to be systematized and organised, that is, edited, classified, and tabulated. Here, editing implies the checking of gathered data for accuracy, utility, and completeness; classifying refers to the dividing of the information into different catagories, classes or heads for use; and tabulating denotes the recording of the classified material in accurate mathematical terms, for example, marking and counting frequency tallies for different items on which information is gathered.

The data, for the present study on achievement of secondary school students in Social Studies, was analysed keeping in view the objectives and hypotheses of the study. The marks of Social Studies of tenth class public examinations were taken as raw scores for each candidate. These raw scores were used as the basic source of data and were put to statistical treatment.

The maximum score a student can get was 100 and the minimum was 1. In the present study, the highest score secured by a student was 82 and the lowest was 6.

For classification of the scores into low, average, and high achievement groups, the pupil who scored 30 and below was kept in low achievement group, who scored between 31 and 60 was kept in average group and who scored 60 and above was kept in high achievement group, based on normal probability distribution.

The mean scores were considered to compare the sub-sample variation in achievement levels.

The values of standard deviation were applied to identify the dispersion of scores in each case of the sample.

The chi-square (χ^2) test of independence was used for computing the experimentally obtained results with those to be expected on a hypothesis. The hypotheses formulated for this study were accordingly rejected or accepted.

The following are the processes of data analysis and their findings.

Hypothesis 1. The secondary school pupils will possess a high achievement in Social Studies.

To test the validity of hypothesis 1, the following calculations were attended.

Table 3 : Level of Social Studies Achievement in the Whole Sample

Sample	Mean	Standard Deviation
300	48·24	18·42

As per the mean score value the achievement of secondary school pupils in Social Studies was average. The scores in the whole sample were also distributed diversely.

It is further tried to know the distribution of Social Studies achievement in the whole sample.

Table 4 : Distribution of Social Studies Achievement in the Whole Sample

Sample		Low	Average	High	χ^2
300	f_o	51	164	85	36·54*
	f_e	48	204	48	

* Significant at 0.01 level

fo = frequency of occurrence of observed facts

fe = frequency of occurrence of some hypothesis

The achievement in Social Studies was not normal. Its trend was towards high achievement though its main concentration was in average category.

The hypothesis that "the secondary school pupils will possess high achievement in Social Studies" can be rejected.

Hypothesis 2. There will be a significant difference in Social Studies achievement between boys and girls of secondary schools.

A comparison was made to identify the difference in Social Studies achievement of secondary school boys and girls.

Table 5 : Comparison of Social Studies Achievement Boys and Girls

Variable	*Sample*	*Mean*	*Standard Deviation*	*Mean Difference*	*Critical Ratio*
Boys	150	48·44	18·45	0·06	36·13*
Girls	150	48·50	18·30		

* Significant at 0.01 level

As per the mean scores, there was no difference in the Social Studies achievement between boys and girls. The achievement was average in both cases. There was a high dispersion of scores in both the cases.

Statistical treatment was further given to the data to identify the level of distribution in boys and girls.

Table 6: Distribution of Social Studies achievement in boys and girls.

Variable	*Sample*		*Low*	*Average*	*High*	χ^2
Boys	150	f_o	25	85	40	13.53*
		f_e	24	102	24	
Girls	150	f_o	36	80	44	21.56*
		f_e	24	102	24	

* Significant at 0.01 level

The Social Studies achievement in boys and girls was concentrated in average category. In both the cases the achievement trend was towards high achievement category.

The hypothesis that "there will be a difference in Social Studies achievement between boys and girls of secondary schools" can be rejected.

Hypothesis 3: There will be a significant difference in Social Studies achievement between the pupils of private and government secondary schools.

To test the validity of hypothesis 3, a comparison was made to identify the difference between both the cases.

Table 7: Comparison of Social Studies Achievement of the Pupils of Private and Government Schools

Variable	*Sample*	*Mean*	*Standard Deviation*	*Mean Difference*	*Critical Ratio*
Private	150	60·7	18·54	21·3	2·19*
Govt.	150	35·4	19·44		

* Significant at 0.01 level

There was a great difference in Social Studies achievement between the pupils of private and government secondary schools. The pupils of private schools were with a high achievement. But the pupils of government schools were with low-average achievement. The critical ratio also states the difference between the sub-samples.

Chi-square test was applied to study the distribution of achievement in the sub-samples.

Table 8 : Distribution of Social Studies Achievement in the Pupils of Private and Government Schools.

Variable	*Sample*		*Low*	*Average*	*High*	χ^2
Private	150	f_o	5	74	71	114·76*
		f_e	24	102	24	
Govt.	150	f_o	46	90	14	25.73*
		f_e	24	102	24	

* Significant at 0.01 level

The distribution of Social Studies achievement in the pupils of private and government secondary schools was not normal, as per the chi-square values. The achievement concentration was towards high achievement category in private school pupils, where as it was towards low achievement category in government school pupils.

The hypothesis that "there will be a significant difference in Social Studies achievement between the pupils of private and government secondary schools" can be accepted.

Hypothesis 4 : There will be a significant difference in Social Studies achievement between the pupils of urban and rural secondary schools.

A comparison was made to identify the difference in the level of Social Studies achievement between the pupils of urban and rural schools.

Table 9: Comparison of Social Studies Achievement of the Pupils of Urban and Rural Schools

Variable	*Sample*	*Mean*	*Standard Deviation*	*Mean Difference*	*Critical Ratio*
Urban	150	61·5	20·18	14·4	0·56*
Rural	150	47·1	24·75		

* Significant at 0.01 level

There was a significant difference in Social Studies achievement between urban and rural pupils. The urban pupils possessed a high achievement and the rural pupils an average achievement.

Necessary computations were made to know the distribution of Social Studies achievement in the two sub-samples.

Table 10 : Distribution of Social Studies Achievement in Urban and Rural Pupils.

Variable	*Sample*		*Low*	*Average*	*High*	χ^2
Urban	150	f_o	25	79	46	25·38*
		f_e	24	102	24	
Rural	150	f_o	26	85	39	12.36*
		f_e	24	102	24	

* Significant at 0.01 level

The achievement distribution in the sub-samples was not normal. In case of urban pupils, the achievement concentration was slightly tending towards high category, but it's main concentration in rural pupils was in average category.

The hypothesis that "there will be a significant difference in the Social Studies achievement between the pupils of rural and urban secondary schools" can be accepted.

5

SUMMARY, CONCLUSIONS AND DISCUSSION

Social Studies is the branch of study which deals with man, his relations with other men and his environment. Its content is drawn from several social sciences and bears a direct relationship with the purposes for which it is taught. Broadly speaking, these purposes include an understanding of human relations, knowledge of the surrounding environment, dedication to the basic principles and values of the society in which it is taught, and a commitment to participation in the processes through which that society is maintained and improved.

Social Studies is a compulsory and one of the important subjects upto secondary level, taught either as Environmental Studies or as Social Studies. The pupils who pursue Social Studies of quite a long time must have a good command over the subject, which helps them achieve well in their examinations. Hence, a study has been undertaken to study the achievement in Social Studies of secondary school pupils.

The objectives of the present study are— 1. To find out the achievement of secondary school pupils in Social Studies, 2. To compare the Social Studies achievement of boys and girls, urban and rural pupils, and government and private school pupils.

Considering their role in determining the Social Studies achievement, variables such as boys versus girls, urban versus rural pupils, and government versus private school pupils are considered for this study.

The hypotheses formulated for this study considering the variables and objectives are— The secondary school pupil will possess a high achievement in Social Studies, and There will be a significant difference in Social Studies achievement between boys and girls, urban and rural pupils and the pupils of government and private secondary school.

A sample of 300 tenth class pupils are selected as sample through stratified random sampling technique. Random sampling was also applied to select units from each stratum. Equal weightage is given to boys and girls, pupils of private and government schools, and pupils of urban and rural schools.

The marks scored in tenth class public examination conducted by the Board of Secondary Education, Government of Andhra Pradesh have been taken as raw scores to measure the achievement in Social Studies.

CONCLUSIONS AND DISCUSSION

The present study has yielded the following conclusions for discussion.

"The pupils of secondary schools possessed an average achievement in Social Studies."

The achievement of the secondary school pupils in Social Studies is not much encouraging. The causes for this unsatisfactory achievement may be many and multidimensional. Many researchers have identified the intelligence, adjustment, creativity, values, motivation, study habits, attitude towards the subjects, socio economic status, parents education, etc., as some of the correlates of achievement. Besides the above correlates, the efficiency of teachers, the well equipped libraries, the conducive teaching learning atmosphere, the use of audio visual teaching aids, the administration, the institutional characteristics, the efforts put in by the students to learn Social Studies will also play their legitimate role in enhancing the academic achievement. So the possible factors among these should be implemented in our secondary schools to make the students achieve well in Social Studies.

"There was no difference in the achievement of Social Studies between boys and girls. Both these groups secured an average achievement only."

Certain studies identified a difference between boys and girls in academic achievement. In some cases boys fared well and in some others the girls scored well. But this study did not show any difference in Social Studies achievement between boys and girls. As the facilities are equal to both boys and girls there was no difference in achievement. The samples—girls and boys—were brawn from the co-educational institutions and this might have been contributed for the non-difference in achievement. Whatever the reasons may be, this is a good sign and the facilities—from parents and institutions side—must be equally extended to both boys and girls. Both boys and girls must try to improve their achievement status by putting all their efforts in learning and presenting the subject at need.

"The pupils of private secondary schools scored well than the pupils of government schools. The private school pupils' achievement in Social Studies was high and the government school pupils' achievement was average. The achievement concentration trend was tending towards high achievement in case of private school pupils and it was towards low achievement in government school pupils."

Almost every study on achievement shows that the pupils of private educational institutions were scoring well than their counter-parts and this study has no exception. The private institutions are famous for their educational facilities such as infrastructure library, learning, and teaching. These will contribute to a major extent for better achievement. As the private schools are managed efficiently and as the management in readily available to look after every education phenomenon, the achievement-whatever its status may be- of students will be taken care of. When the low or average achievement is questioned immediately, everyone concerned will take responsibility of it and work hard for better achievement. The students will also attend to the educational activities with utmost responsibility under the constant supervision of teachers and management. These things lack in government schools and the result is poor achievement. So the feasible facilities and effective administration should be there in government schools also to enhance academic achievement.

"The urban pupils scored very well than the rural pupils in Social Studies. The urban pupils secured a high achievement in Social Studies and their counter-parts got an average achievement"

The urban schools are famous for their facilities. Every possible effort will be put in by schools, parents and pupils in urban areas to secure high achievement. There will be a heavy competition among urban schools and students in every aspect so as to keep themselves in pace with others. Above all, most, of the schools in urban areas are managed by private agencies and the educational, economical and social backgrounds of the parents and pupils in urban areas will also be high. The rural atmosphere in entirely different. The schools are mostly managed by government bodies and the pupils also study at their leisure time without much stress and charm as they do not aspire much and as they lack any competition. The parents also take education in a light secure as they enjoy in farming even though they face hardships in socio-economic conditions. Everyone is familiar with the available facilities and teachers' efficiency of government schools. The scene has to change in rural areas and the pupils must go along with urban ones in every aspect. For this, the government, teachers and parents must extend their full support to the rural children. There must be a very good learning atmosphere in all types of educational institutions irrespective of place and time.

To conclude, the achievement in Social Studies was average in the whole sample. Boys and girls, pupils of government schools and rural pupils secured an average achievement, but the pupils of urban and private schools secured a high achievement. Sex did not play any role in achievement. Everyone one concerned should take care of this achievement and even effort must be put in to improve the present status of achievement in Social Studies.

SUGGESTIONS FOR FURTHER RESEARCH

The researchers may consider the following areas for their investigations.

1. Studies may be conducted on Social Studies achievement at different levels.
2. Studies may be carried out to find out the effect

of independent variables on dependent variables in the cases of controlled and experimental groups.

3. Studies may be taken up to measure the effect of psycho-social variables on achievement in Social Studies.
4. Studies may be conducted to identify this level of achievement at secondary school level/other levels.
5. Studies may be considered related to the role of fairs, exhibitions, tours, direct experiences, etc., in enhancing the academic achievement.

BIBLIOGRAPHY

Aggarwal, J.C.. (1983). *Teaching of History.* New Delhi : Vikas Publishing House.

American Historical Association (1939). *Commission on the Social Studies : Conclusions and Recommendations.* New York: AHA.

Anastasi, A. (1961). *Psychological Testing.* New York. MacMillan Co.

Beard, C.A. (1934). "The Nature of the Social Studies", in *Report of the Commission of Social Studies.* New York: American Historical Association.

Best, John W. (1982). *Research in Education.* New Delhi: Prentice-Hall of India.

Bhaskara Rao, D. (1982). *An Evaluative Study of the New Science Curriculum at Upper Primary Level in Andhra Pradesh.* Master of Education Dissertation, Nagarjuna University.

Bhaskara Rao. D. (1983 July). "Teacher: The Supreme of Mankind". *Education.* 63: 193-196.

Bhaskara Rao. D. (1984 February). "Private Educational Institutions". *The Educational Review.* XC : 34-36.

Bhaskara Rao, D. (1985. August). "Effective Communication in Teaching". *Experiments in Education* XIII : 109-111.

Bhaskara Rao. D. (1986. February). "Utilization of Community Resources in Science Teaching" *Junior Scientist.* 23: 5-6.

Bhaskara Rao, D. (1989). *A Comparative Study of Scientific Attitude, Scientific Aptitude and Achievement in Biology at Secondary School Level.* PH.D. Thesis, Osmania University.

Bhaskara Rao, D. (1989). *Dhrusya Sravana Bhodhapanakaranamulu* (Audio Visual Teaching Aids). Guntur: Nagarjuna Publishers.

Bhaskara Rao, D. (1989. October). "Objectives of Science" *Science Promoter*, 2: 701-703.

Bhaskara Rao, D, (1991, September 16-18) "Biological Basis of Learning". Second INTERNATIONAL Conference on *Differentiated Psychology of Learning—Its Fundamentals and Application*, Martin Luther University, Halle, Germany.

Bhaskara Rao, D. (1992. August 2-8). "Teaching Learning Strategies in Environmental Education". *Eight Asian Symposium of International Council of Associations for Science Education* on *Science Education for a Changing World.* International Council of Association for Science Education. Colombo, Srilanka.

Bhaskara Rao, D. (1992. July 8-14). "Quality or Equality". *Eight Congress of World Council of Comparative Education Societies* on *Education, Democracy and Development.* Charles University, Prague, Czechosiovakia.

Bhaskara Rao, D. (1992, May 11-15). "Scientific Attitude in Secondary School Pupil". *Second International Conference* on *History and Philosophy of Science and Science Teaching.* Queen's University, Kingston, Ontario, Canada.

Bhaskara Rao, D. (1992. October 11-14). "Underachievement: Identification, Diagnosis and Treatment". *Third European Conference of the European Council for High Ability on Competence and Responsibility.* University of Munich, Munich, Germany.

Bhaskara Rao, D. (1993). *Viganaasasthra Bodhana* (Teaching of Science). Guntur: Nagarjuna Publishers.

Bhaskara Rao, D. (1993, August 20-25). "Development of Educational Television in India". International Conference Teleteaching 93 on *Learning and Working Independent of Time and Distance* . Foundation for Continuing Education of the Norwegian Institute of Technology, Trondheim, Norway.

Bhaskara Rao, D. (1993. January 3-8). "Teacher's role in dealing with Learning Difficulties". *International Conference* on *Science Education in Developing Countries:* ***From Theory to Practice***. The Amos De-Shalit Israeli Science Teaching Centre, Jerusalem, Israel.

Bhaskara Rao, D. (1993. November 11-14). "Education for Peace- Need of the Day". Second Conference of the European Peace Research Association on *Improving European Security: Threats and Responsibilities*. Budapest, Hungary.

Bhaskara Rao, D. (1993, October 1-4). "Disarmament". Fifth International Castiglioncello Conference on *Conflicts and Disarmament*. Union of Scientists for Disarmament. Italy.

Bhaskara Rao, D. (1993, September 5-9). "Education vis-a-vis Democracy". Fourth School Year 2020 Conference. *The European Educational House*. IMTEC & COMED. Bogensee, Germany.

Bhaskara Rao, D. (1994). *Jeevasasthra Bodhana* (Teaching of Biology). Guntur: Creative Press.

Bhaskara Rao, D. (1994). *Scientific Aptitude*. New Delhi: Ashish Publishing House.

Bhaskara Rao, D. (1994, April 6-9). "Creativity and Academic Achievement". European Council for High Ability's International Workshop on *Creative Potential-Exploring and Developing*. University degli studi di Pavic. Pavia, Italy.

Bhaskara Rao, D. (1994, October 8-11). "Special Activities for Talented in General Classes". Fourth Conference of the European Council for High Ability on *Nurturing Talent: Individual Needs and Social Ability*. University of Nijmegen, Nijmegen, The Netherlands.

Bhaskara Rao, D. (1995). *Vidya Manovignana Sasthram* (Educational Psychology). Guntur: Creative Press.

Bhaskara Rao, D. and D. Pushpa Latha (1994). *Achievement in Biology*. New Delhi: Discovery Publishing House.

Bhaskara Rao, D. and C. Sridevi (1994, October). "A Comparative Study of Mathematics Achievement and Educational Aspirations of Intermediate Students with reference to their association with Each other". *Journal of Educational Research and Extension* 31: 109-117.

Bhaskara Rao, Digumarti (1994, November 24-27). "Administrative Leadership in Educational Enterprises". The Fifth International Seminar of Educational Leadership International on *Educational Leadership and Social Changes*, Tallinn Pedagogical University, Tallinn Estonia.

Bhaskara Rao, D. (1995, July 30- August 5). "Non-violent Means to Combat Violence in Education". The 1995 World Congress of Parents. Teachers and Students for Social Responsibility on *We The Peoples... Educating for a World Without Violence*, Norwich University, Northfield, Vermont United States of America.

Bhaskara Rao, D. (1995, July 30 August 4). "Enhancing Academic Achievement". The 11th World Conference on Gifted and Talented Children on *Maximising Potential: Lengthening and Strengthening our Stride*, Hong Kong.

Bhaskara Rao, D. and B. Veena Kumari (1995). *Operation Blackboard*. New Delhi: Ashish Publishing House.

Bhaskara Rao, D. and D. Pushpa Latha (1995). *Achievement in English*. New Delhi: Discovery Publishing House.

Bhaskara Rao, D. and D. Pushpa Latha (1995). *Achievement in Mathematics*. New Delhi: Discovery Publishing House.

Bhaskara Rao, D. and D. Pushpa latha (1995). *Achievement in Science*. New Delhi: Discovery Publishing House.

Bhaskara Rao, D. and K. Vijaya (1995). *A Text book Evaluation*. Ambala Cantt: The Associated Publishers.

Bhaskara Rao, Digumarti (1995). *Scientific Attitude*.

Bining, C.A. and H.D. Bining (1935). *Teaching the Social Studies in Secondary Schools*. New Delhi: Tata McGraw-Hill Publishing Co. Ltd.

Biswas, A. and J.C. Aggarwal (1987). *Encyclopedic Dictionary and Directory of Education*. New Delhi: The Academic Publishers (India).

Biswas, A. and S. Aggarwal (1987). *Indian Educational Documents since Independence*. New Delhi: The Academic Publishers (India).

Bhandwein, Paul F. Fletcher G. Watson and Paul E. Blackwood (1958). *A Book of Methods*. New York: Harcourt, Brace & World Inc.

Buch, M.B. ed. (1979). *Second Survey of Research in Education*. Baroda: Society for Educational Research and Development.

Buch M.B. Chief ed. (1987). *Third Survey of Research in Education*. New Delhi: National Council of Educational Training and Research.

Carter V. Good, ed. (1973). *Dictionary of Education*. New York: McGraw-Hill Book Co.

Choudary, K.P. (1975). *Effective Teaching of History in India*. New Delhi: National Council of Educational Research and Training.

David G. Armstrong (1980). *Social Studies in Secondary Education*. New York: MacMillan Publishing Company, Inc.

Desai, D.B. and A. Govind (1979). *Studies in Achievement Motivation*. Baroda: Centre for Advanced Studies in Education, M.S. University of Baroda.

Digumarti (1994, JANUARY). "The Mind". *Science Promoter*. 7: 4-9

Dunfee, M. and M. Sagh (1966). *Social Studies Through Problem Solving*. New York: Holt, Rinehart and Winston, Inc.

English, H.B. and A.C. English (1958). *A Comprehensive Dictionary of Psychoanalytical Terms*. London: Longmans.

Festinger, Leon and Katz Daniel (1976). *Research methods in the Behavioural Science*. New Delhi: Amerind Publishing Co.

Freeman, Frank S. (1965). *Theory and Practice of Psychological Testing*. Calcutta: Oxford & IBH Publishing Co.

Gage, N.L. (1966). *Handbook of Research on Teaching*. Chicago: Rand McNally & Co.

Garret, Henry E. (1979). *Statistics in Psychology and Education*. Bombay: Peffer and Simons Pvt. Ltd.

Good, C.V., ed. (1959). *Dictionary of Education*. New York: McGraw-Hill Book Co.

Goode, William J. and Paul K. Hatt (1983). *Methods in Social Research*. Tokyo : McGraw-Hill International Book Co.

High, J. (1962). *Teaching Secondary School Social Studies*. New York : John Willy and Sons, Inc.

Jayaswall, Sita Ram (1968). *Techniques and Tests in Psychology and Education*. Lucknow : Prakashan Kendra.

Kerlinger, Fred N. (1964). *Foundations of Behavioural Research*. Holt, Rinehart & Winston.

Khasnaris, P.K. (1983). *Teaching of Social Studies in India*. New Delhi : Abhinav Publications.

Kochhar (1984). *Teaching of Social Studies.* New Delhi : Sterling Publishers Pvt. Ltd.

Ministry of Human Resource Development, Department of Education, Government of India (1985). Challenges *of Education: A Policy Perspective.*

Ministry of Human Resource Development, Department of Education, Government of India (1986). *National Policy on Education-1986.*

Moffat, Mawrice P. (1954). *Social Studies Instruction: Organising, Teaching and Supervising Social Studies in Secondary Schools.* Englewood Clifts, New Jersy: Prentice-Hall, Inc.

Mukherjee, Radha Kumud (1947). *Ancient Indian Education.* London: MacMillan company.

National Scheme of Inservice Training of School Teachers (1987). *Resource Material General.* New Delhi: NCERT.

National Scheme of Inservice Training of School Teachers (1987). *Resource Material-Primary.* New Delhi: NCERT.

National Scheme of Inservice Training of School Teachers (1987). *Resource Material-Secondary.* New Delhi: NCERT.

Programme of Mass Orientation for School Teachers (1988). *Inservice Teacher Education Package, Vol 1: For Primary School Teachers.* New Delhi: NCERT.

Programme of Mass Orientation for School Teachers (1988). *Inservice Teacher Education Package, Vol 2: For Secondary School Teachers.* New Delhi: NCERT.

Rathiah, L. and D. Bhaskara Rao (1994, November). "Achievement of Intermediate Students in Residential and Non-residential Junior Colleges with Reference to Socio-Economic Status, Educational Aspirations and Adjustment" *The Educational Review* C: 189-194.

Rathaiah, L. and D. Bhaskara Rao (1995). *Achievement Correlates.* Ambala Cantt. The Indian Publications.

Rawat, P.L. (1976). *History of Indian Education.* Agra: Ram Prasad and Sons.

Reader's Digest (1984). *Great Illustrated Dictionary.* London: The Readers Digest Association Ltd.

Report of the Education Commission, 1964-66. *Education and National Development.* New Delhi: NCERT.

Report of the Secondary Education Commission, 1952-53. Government of India.

Rummel, J. Francis (1958). *An Introduction to Research Procedures in Education.* New York: Harper and Brothers.

Singh, Raja Roy (1986). *Education in Asia and the Pacific-Retrospect: Prospect.* Bangkok: UNESCO Regional Office for Education in Asia and the Pacific.

Social Studies—A Draft Syllabus for Classes 1 To XI (1973). New Delhi: NCERT.

Smith, Edward W., Stahely W. Kroure, Jr. and Mark M. Atkinson (1967). *The Educator's Encyclopedia,* Englewwood Cliffs: Prentice Hall, Inc.

Srinivas, Bhattacharya and D.R. Darji (1966). *Teaching Social Studies in Indian Schools.* Baroda: Acharya Book Depot.

Stermzand, M.J. and Rocurt H. Lewis (1935). *New Methods in Social Studies.* New York: Farrer and Rinehart.

Sukhia, S.P., P.V. Mehrotra and R.N. Mehrotra (1980). *Elements of Educational Research.* New Delhi: Allied Publishers Pvt. Ltd.

Teaching Social Studies (1969). New Delhi. NCERT.

The Curriculum For the Ten Year School (1975). New Delhi: NCERT.

Venkata Rao, P. and D. Bhaskara Rao (1989). *A Text Book of Zoology—Junior Intermediate,* Revised Edition. Guntur: Vigyan Publishers.

Venkata Rao, P. and D. Bhaskara Rao (1989). *A Text Book of Zoology- Senior Intermediate,* Revised Edition. Guntur: Vigyan Publishers.

Vidya, Ratna Taneja (1970). *Fundamentals of Teaching Social Studies.* Chandigarh: Mohindra Capital Publishers.

Weslay, C.B. (1950). *Teaching of Social Studies in High Schools.* Boston: D. C. Health and Company.

Wesley, C.B. and Stanley Wronski (1973). *Teaching Secondary Social Studies in a World Society.* Lenington, Mass: D.C. Health and Company.

Yajnik, K.S. (1966). *The Teaching of Social Studies in India.* Bombay: Orient Longmans Ltd.

APPENDIXES

Board of Secondary Education

Government of Andhra Pradesh

Secondary School Certificate Course

Social Studies

Paper 1 — History & Civics

Time : 2½hrs.] [Max. Marks: 50]

Time :2 Hrs.] [Marks : 37]

PART-A

SECTION-1

Note : (i) Answer any SIX of the following not exceeding 5 lines each.

(ii) Each question carries 2 marks. 6 × 2 = 12

1. What is a Revolution? When do Revolutions occur?
2. Which was called as the 'Indian National Congress'? When was it started?
3. What are the achievements oi moderates?
4. What is known as 'Simon Commission'?
5. What is 'non-alignment'?
6. 'Preamble is not a part of the Constitution'. Why?
7. Where does the president of India reside?
8. What are the Elective powers of the Parliament?
9. On what grounds can the Governor of a State be removed from office?
10. Why is local-sell government introduced in the administration of our country?

SECTION -II (HISTORY)

Note : (i) Answer any TWO of the following not exceeding 10 lines each.

(ii) Each question carries 5 marks. 2×5=10

11. Explain the growth of Democracy in England.
12. What are the lessons of French Revolution?
13. What were the economic causes for the First World War?
14. Write about the nationalist struggle in Namibia.
15. Explain the achievements made by India after Independence.

SECTION - III (CIVICS)

Note : (i) Answer any Two of the following not exceeding 10 lines each.

(ii) Each question carries 5 marks. 2×5=10

16. 'The Constitution of India establishes a Parliamentary system of Government at the Centre and in the States'. How?
17. Explain the difference between the Lok Sabha and the Rajya Sabha.
18. What is the composition of a High Court?
19. What are sources of Revenue to the village panchayats.
20. Describe the role of U.N.O. in maintaining world peace.

SECTION-IV

Note: (i) Answer any ONE of the following.

(ii) The question carries 5 marks. 5

21. On the given outline map of Africa, mark the following: (1) Zimbabwe (2) Nigeria (3) Mali (4) Morocco (5) Senegal
22. On the given outline map of Europe mark the following: (1) France (2) England (3) Italy (4) Norway (5) Austria

---

Time : 30 Mts.] **PART-B** [Marks:13

Note: (i) Answer ALL questions.

(ii) Each question carries ½ mark.

1. Choose the correct answer:

1. Which of the following is known as 'Mother of Parliaments'? ( )

(A) Indian Parliament
(B) French Parliament
(C) American Parliament
(D) British Parliament

2. Which of the following wars cost England heavily to the tune of £14 crores? ( )
   (A) The First World War
   (B) The Second World War
   (C) The Seven years war
   (D) The Five Years war
3. The fall of Czar is known as ( )
   (A) The incident of 1905
   (B) The incident of 1917
   (C) The February Revolution
   (D) The old Russian Calender
4. The idea of the use of 'Swadeshi' goods was popularised by ( )
   (A) Mahatma Gandhi
   (B) Pandit Jawaharlal Nehru
   (C) The Indian National Congress
   (D) The Early Nationalists
5. The Second World War came to an end on ( )
   (A) 14-08-1945
   (B) 07-08-1945
   (C) 09-08-1945
   (D) None of the above
6. The British Government appointed the Simon Commission in year ( )
   (A) 1905
   (B) 1927
   (C) 1935
   (D) 1846
7. One of the features of Democratic State is ( )
   (A) It is not guided by any particular religion
   (B) It is free in its intenal and external matters
   (C) It gives a positive direction to the Government in fromulating its policies
   (D) The real power of the state emanates from the people.

8. The following enjoys the real execultives authority of the Government ( )
   (A) The President of India
   (B) The Prime Minister
   (C) The Council of Ministers
   (D) The Parliament
9. The Stage Legislature of the following State consists of only one House. ( )
   (A) Andhra Pradesh
   (B) Bihar
   (C) Karnataka
   (D) Maharashtra
10. The Executive Body of the United Nations is ( )
   (A) The General Assembly
   (B) The Security Council
   (C) The Trusteeship Council
   (D) The Secretariat

II. Fill in the blanks:

11. ....was the first country to reverse the trend of 'absolute monarchy'.
12. ....constitution was the first genuine democratic constitution in History.
13. The movement which was led by Mazzini and Garibaldi is known as.............................
14. ....constitution represented a curious blending of the principles of aristocracy and democracy.
15. ....roused through this writings and speeches patriotic spirit in the youth of Italy.
16. ....the Prime Minister of India, attended the conference field at l Tashkant.
17. The Satellite launched by India in June 1981 is called.......................................
18. Planning Commission was put up to draw plans for the economic development of country in the year................
19. Double citizenship is in vogue in ....country.
20. To be elected as President of India the candidate should have completed............... years of age.

21. Suspending a sentence of punishment given by any court by the President of India comes under.............powers vested by the President.
22. ....as a leader of nation speaks to the world on behalf of the country.
23. The total number of states in the country are........
24. The ex-officio chairman of the Rajya Sabha is........
25 The head of the Zilla Praja Parishad is known as.......
26. The United Nations organisation came into existence on..........

SOCIAL STUDIES

Paper 2—Geography & Economics

Time: 2½hrs] **[Max. Marks: 50**

Time: 2Hrs.] **PART-A** [Marks : 37

SECTION-1

Note: (i) Answer any SIX of the following not exceeding 5 lines each.

(ii) Each question carries 2 marks. *6 x 2 = 12*

1. What are the parallel zones of Himalayas?
2. "A good climate of a place is considered to be a natural resource for the people living in it" Substantiate.
3. What is the difference between productive forestry and social forestry?
4. Which are the dependable sources of energy? How are they dependable?
5. What should be the exports and imports in a country? Why?
6. What were the strains and stresses faced by our country during the Second Five Year Plan period?
7. Write any four important measures taken in Fifth and Sixth Five Year Plans to uplift rural and weaker sections of the society?

8. List Out two special schemes and implemented in the Five Year Plans for the welfare of scheduled castes and scheduled tribes.
9. Suggest any four efforts to be taken to wipe out the gap between the "Haves" and "Havenots".
10. Why did the foreign exchange reserves deplete during the period of Second Five Year Plan?

SECTION-II (GEOGRAPHY)

Note: (i) Answer any Two of the following not exceeding 10 lines each.
(ii) Each question carries 5 marks. *2×5 = 10*

11. State the reason for less rainfall in Punjab and Kashmir and no rainfall in desert of Rajasthan and Ladakh.
12. What are the ill effects of indiscriminate deforestation?
13. Even though our country achieved industrial development, there is still need to develop our agriculture today. Why?
14. What did we learn from Green Revolution?
15. "The efficient transport system gives life to the modern economy". How ?

SECTION-III (ECONOMICS)

Note: (i) Answer any Two of the following not exceeding 10 lines each.
(ii) Each question carries 5 marks. *2×5=10*

16. Why is India called "a rich country inhabited by poor people"? What planned steps were taken to correct this situation?
17. How do you say that the economic situation prevailing in India at the time of independence was deplorable?
18. Write five main elements of Fifth Five Year Plan strategy for removal of poverty and attainment of self-reliance.
19. Give the objectives of the Seventh Five year Plan.
20. List out the social welfare activities undertaken in the Five Year Plans to develop and rehabilitate the weaker sections of the society.

SECTION-IV

Note: (i) Answer any One of the following.

(ii) The question carries 5 marks. 5

21. On the given outline map of India, mark the following:

    (1) Mahanadi with Hirakud dam,

    (2) River Sutlej with Bhakra dam.

22. On the given outline map of India, locate the following parts:

    (1) New Mangalore (2) Kandla (3) Paradeep (4) Tuticorin (5) Cochin

PART-B

Time:30 mts.] [Marks:13

Note: (i) Answer ALL questions,

(ii) Each question carries ½ mark.

1. Choose the correct answer;

   1. Which one among the following summer resorts is not in Himalyas? ( )

      (A) Nainital
      (B) Ooty
      (C) Darjeeling
      (D) Mussorie

   2. Which one among the following is not a tributary of the river Ganga? ( )

      (A) Ganga
      (B) Gandak
      (C) Sarda
      (D) Rabi

   3. South-east trace winds deflect to the right after crossing the equator because ( )

      (A) They blow from the high pressure belt
      (B) They blow towards the low pressure belt
      (C) The temperature at the equator is high
      (D) The earth rotates from west to east

   4. The Planning Commission in 1978-79 classified the irrigation projects on the basis of ( )

(A) The cost of the projects
(B) The extent of area irrigated
(C) On the basis of the above two factors
(D) The position of the rivers on which they are constructed

5. Which one of the following is applicable for red soils ( )
(A) Rich in Phosphorous and potash
(B) Rich in iron, lime and nitrogen
(C) Deficient in phosphorous, lime and nitrogen and rich in iron.
(D) Rich in lime, medium and potash but deficient in nitrogen

6. Which one of the following is not a metallic mineral ? ( )
(A) Manganese
(B) Bauxite
(C) Chromite
(D) Graphite

7. Which one among the following is not a critical problem that was faced by Indian Economy during 1914-47? ( )
(A) The two world wars
(B) Freedom struggle
(C) Serious economic depression
(D) Partition of country

8. The First Five Plan which assigned first priority to the development of heavy and basic industries was ( )
(A) First
(B) Second
(C) Third
(D) Fourth

9. Which one among the following is not a factor responsible for the speedy growth of economy in India, as visualized by the planners? ( )
(A) Inflationary rise in prices
(B) Recurrent floods and drought
(C) Devaluation of currency
(D) Population control

10. Which one among the following is not a hurdle in the way of public co-operation ( )

(A) Ignorance of democracy and socialism
(B) Low literacy rate
(C) Chronic economic backwardness
(D) Modern outlook and attitude

II. Fill in the blanks with suitable word or words:

11. Panchamari hills are part............. mountain.
12. The .... river rises near the glacier Gangotri.
13. The retreating south-west monsoons give rain to.............
14. The national policy resolution of 1952 proposed to raise the area under forests to .... to the total land area.
15. The crop which has highest production in our country is.........
16. .... Which belongs to Coorg of Karnataka State is one of the best of Indian cows.
17 Eighty-eight percentage of the total world production of this mineral.........come from India.
18. The Headquarters of North Eastern railway zona is at..........
19. Princess Dock is dock in ....part.
20. The British Government discarded the policy of ....after 1920 and began to prefect Indian industries to a limited extend.
21. A planning commission was appointed in India in the year.................. for the first time.
22. Sindhri Fertilizer factory was established during the................ Five year Plan.
23. The two major objectives of the Fifth Five year Plan were............ and attainment of sell reliance.
24. The literacy rate in our country as per 1991 census is............
25. The economic progress achieved through Five Year Plans is being countered by the growing..............
26. A vast segment of people in India are caught - up in the vicious circle of............... low consumption and low standard of living.